CHOICE AND COMPROMISE

A Woman's Guide to Balancing Family and Career

Donna N. Douglass

amacom

AMERICAN MANAGEMENT ASSOCIATIONS

To Merrill—
my best friend, who shares my life

and

To my daughters—
the blessings who make each day a joy

Library of Congress Cataloging in Publication Data

Douglass, Donna N.
    Choice and compromise.

    Bibliography: p.
    Includes index.
    1. Women—United States—Social conditions.
2. Women—Employment—Social aspects—United States.
3. Housewives—United States—Psychology.   I. Title.
HQ1426.D819   1983   305.4'2   82–73513
ISBN 0–8144–5746–0

First Printing

Acknowledgments

With each thought and word in this book, I became increasingly aware of how dependent we all are on each other. So many people contributed to the ideas expressed here; many of them are unaware of their contribution.

I drew heavily on the experience of the women in my life; their lives gave perspective to my own. My grandmothers, Elvera and Mathilda, are both strong-minded yet loving women, and I appreciate their legacy.

My mother, Ruth, is a gentle lady who had the wisdom and courage to let me be me. My look-alike sister, Diane, 21 years my junior, has given me the unusual opportunity of watching "myself" grow up again in a different world. She provides a perspective my own children do not.

My stepdaughters, Debbie, Donna, and Susan, have also been important to me. They were part of my husband's other life but have now become the pluses of my life.

My own daughter, Jennifer, truly opened my eyes to life's process. It was a big job for one so little, but she continues to make me aware of the wonders of this world. And now my unborn baby brings me renewed curiosity for what is yet to be.

Four generations of men have also been significant. Both my grandfathers, Albert and Edward, have been examples of dignity, grace, humor, and gentleness.

My father, Donald, was my teacher throughout the years of my childhood, always challenging me to be all I could be. He gave me the priceless gift of feeling worthwhile, and for this special attitude I will forever be in his debt.

My husband, Merrill, is a constant source of challenge and encouragement. He listens eagerly to my dreams and plans—and then asks me the date I'll finish them! He demands a lot and shares my joy when I produce more than I ever thought was possible.

My brothers, Rich, Doug, Roger, and Ron, have fought with me, differed with me, and loved me. They've helped make me tough. They continue to be an important part of me, no matter how many miles separate us.

My stepson, Steve, has also been a significant factor in my life. Of the children whom I've mothered since preschool years, he is the first to approach adulthood, and he has contributed as much to my growth as I have to his.

iii

There were also many women who have shared their life's joys and frustrations with me over coffee, in airports, on beaches, in classes, and in restaurants, but I particularly want to acknowledge the hundreds of women who took the time to respond to my questionnaires. I cried, smiled, and rejoiced with all of you. You will always be my friends.

Donna N. Douglass

Contents

PART I
WOMAN HERSELF

1

CAUGHT IN THE MIDDLE

A MONDAY MORNING CALL

"This is Meg Johnson," a voice said to me on the phone. "I called because I thought you might be able to help me. I'm a staff nurse at Hope Hill Psychiatric Hospital across town, and I'm putting together a seminar for some of the women patients here. Nothing really elaborate, you understand—I don't have time for all that—just some general thoughts on setting goals and priorities. Maybe a few time tips."

"Sure, Meg," I responded. "I've been dealing with women's issues for some time now; maybe I can help. What sorts of problems do these women have?"

"Well, these patients are really under a lot of stress," Meg explained. "Most of them are working women. They have demanding jobs, with a home to run as well. Some of them have several children to care for, too, so they spend a lot of time running to lessons, helping with homework, settling squabbles, going to the doctor—you know, 'kid work.' To make things worse, their husbands don't seem to understand; they wonder what all the fuss is about. Some of the husbands feel, 'you wanted to work, so you're getting what you asked for.' Other husbands are urging them to work harder so they can get a promotion and earn more money. Most of these women are just plain burned out! They're here in the hospital for only a short period, but I thought maybe I could help."

I sat silently for a few seconds and looked at the papers on my desk. Meg's request for quick ideas hung in the air. Those papers were the responses from the initial questionnaires I had sent out to women all over the country. Some women had only enough time for a one-paragraph reply, while others wrote pages and pages, revealing themselves. Some sounded contented and happy, but most expressed total frustration, both personally

3

and professionally. Their complaints reminded me of those from the women in the psychiatric hospital; I had heard many of these laments before:

> After work, I find it difficult to become a regenerated person. I guess I'm just a born procrastinator!

> I'm unable to relax, so I eat too much. I just have not learned to judge when there is too much stress!

> I have so much to do at home that I end up doing nothing—and feeling frustrated about it. I just turn on the tube and "blah out," or I call someone on the phone and complain about all the work I have to do!

> I want to have a baby, but I believe moms should be with their babies for at least two years after the child is born. My boss is scared to death I'll get pregnant, but the decision is on my shoulders, and time is running out!

> My husband has to work more than 40 hours a week, and I sometimes find myself resenting the amount of time this takes from his presence at home and the amount of help he can give me.

> I mentally take my work home with me. It's really frustrating being "under the gun" both at home and at work!

> My superwoman complex is going to kill me! I think my house should be perfect, my job should be perfect, my kids should be perfect, etc.

> My husband and I don't have time for sex. Everything else seems to come first. We go away from time to time for an evening or a weekend, but I miss at-home time with him!

> There's not enough time for me, and I'm frustrated. I take too much time cleaning the house, and I nag!

> There are seven of us living in a house with 880 square feet of space and one bath. I get one daughter up at 4:45, and the rest start getting up after that. I orchestrate a madhouse!

Meg was still waiting for my response. "Donna," she said as my thoughts focused again on her instead of the questionnaires, "I really don't need much. Do you have any quick ideas?"

"Meg," I began, "I think what you're doing is great. I know these women need help, and I'm glad to see someone making an effort. Yes, I have some things I can send you. I'll put them in the mail this afternoon; but, Meg, these quick tips are like putting a Band-Aid on cancer! They can't do a lot of good, because the problems are so complex. Be sure to tell those overworked patients of yours they aren't alone. They have a lot of company all over this country and probably throughout the world. Maybe it will make them feel better to realize millions of women understand their problems and feel the tensions, too."

Meg thanked me, saying she'd be expecting my materials. I thumbed through my questionnaires a while longer, still thinking of Meg's comment, "These patients are really under a lot of stress." I looked through the respondents' statements about their jobs. Some were very pleased with their work, usually the ones with high-paying jobs and significant responsibilities. Other comments reflected less-than-contented attitudes:

> I want more responsibility—all I'm given are boring, insignificant tasks. I get bogged down; these dinky jobs make me tired and unproductive.

> I'm underpaid; my ideas are not valued enough. I definitely do not have enough time in the day to finish everything.

> Last week, after two martinis, my boss "felt me up"; I was so mad I couldn't see straight!

> I have to spend a lot of time doing clerical work even though I have a management position. My secretarial skills are a problem.

> I feel amazingly guilty if I don't put in a 9- or 10-hour day with an occasional weekend. I wish I felt more comfortable delegating.

> They think I'm cute! They don't take me seriously!

> My boss treats me with respect. All the other men at work are used to women only as mothers, wives, and so on and are amazingly insensitive to women as professionals.

> I hate being a waitress and second wife to my boss. I'm kept so busy doing all his personal chores that I do not have time to do anything for myself.

> I'm not delegating enough. Women are more often used to being the *recipients* of delegation.

> I'm advancing, but the other women see me as a glorified secretary.

> I'm the only female manager in a company with 149 male managers; I must compete with men who can work until ten at night if necessary and still have clean clothes waiting.

Yes, the burned-out patients in that psychiatric hospital have lots of company. Women all over this country are scrambling to run two lives, one at home and one at the shop. They fight tradition, with its nostalgic image of their grandmothers cheerfully stirring the dinner stew with happy babies playing at their feet. From this Norman Rockwell scene, their minds are jerked to another—still idealized—image of reality: the dedicated professional woman who can go through a ten-hour workday and still play a spirited game of squash after preparing a gourmet dinner.

Most of these women couldn't give up their careers if they wanted to. The cost of living is so high that their families depend on their income as well as that of their husbands. Many of them are the sole support of their families; thoughts of staying home are a joke.

But even if they could afford to, many of them wouldn't want to give up their work. They've been told—and they believe—that women who are not gainfully employed outside the home are "unfulfilled." After years of this "liberated" way of thinking, these women would not respect themselves unless they were earning money. Moreover, many of them would be bored if they suddenly decided to "chuck it all" in favor of a domestic calling. One 36-year-old new mother, who decided to stay at home and care for her infant daughter after 15 years of working, put it this way:

> I feel it is really important to be the primary figure in my daughter's life, but at the same time I am aching to be working at a challenging job. I am not happy with housework. It is boring and *not* its own reward. I am happy 80 percent of the time taking care of my child, but it is not always fun.

Women today are definitely "caught in the middle." Their lives are a constant tug-of-war between two selves, and this is more than a casual sense of uneasiness about what they're doing. The decisions women are forced to make can become so maddening that many of them wonder if there can ever be a comfortable resolution. The traditional husband/father has always made choices concerning career, life-styles, values, and directions for the family, but he generally had another person on his team—called a wife. And his duties were always clear: Bring home the bacon and take out the garbage.

The message is clear for women, too: Raise three happy, well-adjusted kids; keep the house spotlessly clean; be ready and willin' whenever your husband is (and initiate it yourself once in a while); be a gourmet cook and hostess extraordinaire; and engage in at least three athletic activities. By the way, also be a corporate executive, skillfully overlooking sexual prejudice and pressures. Do all this with grace and style.

There's only one problem: Doing *all* this is impossible.

Which way does a woman turn? Which is her "real life"? If she chooses to emphasize the wife/mother role, is she following her true calling or being a fool? If she shuns marriage and a family, develops her individual talents to the fullest, and becomes an IBM lawyer, has she made it or missed it all?

A PERSONAL BATTLE

This tug-of-war was made graphically real to me during my twenties and early thirties. I was one of the first crop of postwar babies, born in August 1945. Like many of my generation, I enjoyed a pleasant childhood, happily encouraged by my parents toward an even better future. Of course, I would go to college, even though I was one of six children and my father's income was modest. A college degree was the key to success.

But many of us in college during the 1960s began questioning the goals of postwar America. Vietnam was a factor. Our friends were being shipped off to an unknown country to fight a questionable war. Others, through the college deferment ruling, were enrolled in academic programs they didn't like in order to keep from being drafted. Even those of us who stayed away from the center of antiwar activities were affected by the turmoil around us. The dream was for a better life, but what was better?

The crossroads came for me when I turned 30. After working for a number of years, I returned to college to study for a Ph.D. During this period, I felt there were two totally distinct people who made up "me." One of these people was just like "Phyllis," a fellow Ph.D. candidate a few years younger than I. Phyllis was a tough, no-nonsense woman, dedicated to excellence, competitiveness, and worthwhile causes, particularly the ERA. The idea of Phyllis on a traditional date was as laughable as the thought of her in a dress. She did not play coy politics or games of any sort. She was always serious, always determined to meet her goals.

I mixed well with Phyllis. I was like her in a number of ways, although we realized there were many differences between us. We both had a respect for these differences—and for each other.

But I was also married at the time and living in suburban Atlanta. Most of the women in my neighborhood were homemakers, conducting their lives in a traditional way. During the three summer months, when my young stepchildren came for their yearly visit, I stayed home and "played house." I fed the kids, made beds and dinner, bandaged scratched knees, and bought ice cream. I also joined in neighborhood coffee klatches, sharing housewifely antagonisms, joys, and frustrations. This life was also me. The kids were beautiful and important. *They* were where the real contribution to life was made.

As I grew older, these two separate identities intensified. As a few gray hairs found their way into my brown tresses, my abilities and confidence grew as well. I became competent on a professional level; my goals and opportunities enlarged.

I also had a baby of my own. My father's sudden death had made me vividly aware that life is brief, but the birth of my child showed me that life is constantly renewed. Pregnancy and childbirth were only the beginning of a motherhood adventure that continues to amaze me. How could my "Phyllis" side control me to such an extent that I almost missed having my own child? How could all those women's magazines be *so* wrong about the fulfillment motherhood brings? I almost blew it—by choice!

Now I wanted it *all* and was determined to have it! I wanted to be a total mother and wife; I wanted to be a full-time professional. But how was this possible? I got headaches trying to figure it out. I cried in agreement when I read part of Ann Berk's *Newsweek* essay: "However women play it, there are hard choices to be made that all entail loss—and while that career clock is ticking away, so is the lifeline to the rest of the territory that remains steadfastly theirs."[*]

I continued to read, talk, integrate, and search, and to digest all that was happening around me. I'd question working women and homemakers alike for clues to their frustrations and triumphs. I'd dig for the source of their dismay and the source of their joy. I'd integrate the new information with what I already knew about so many women; and then, one day, I miraculously began to gain some insights. Sense began to grow out of the confusion!

WHAT THIS BOOK CAN DO

There are no clear-cut answers that can be applied to everyone's problems. Each woman has a different set of experiences and a different life, but there are some important truths and guidelines that any woman looking for direction can benefit from today. The major goal of this book is to help every woman who is trying to get off the merry-go-round of ambiguities in order to move ahead. It will:

1. Help you determine where in the middle you are, so you can make the best decisions for your personal and professional life.
2. Share with you the insights and frustrations of women who are in similar situations.
3. Identify the main sources of conflict at home and on the job.
4. Provide you with insights into the attitudes and actions that keep you from being more effective on both the home front and the job front.

---

[*] "Modern Woman's Double Life," *Newsweek*, September 29, 1980, p. 17.

5. Give you workable ideas about handling people and situations that also contribute to confusion and frustration.
6. Provide important suggestions from women who seem to have found the answers for themselves.
7. Show you how to put all these insights together and how to plan for the future.

The call I received from Meg Johnson, the psychiatric nurse, reminds us that this whole business is a little bit crazy. We are on an adventure, for the course is uncharted. We're our own tour guides. We are *one* with those women in Meg Johnson's care, because we are very much a part of them. We have a unity, ladies, because we're all in the same shaky boat. Let's see if we can patch up the sail, catch a wind, and get moving in the right direction!

2
HOW DID WE GET INTO THIS MESS, ANYWAY?

THE SHORT STRAW

"Why did I happen to draw the short straw?" a friend of mine used to say. "If only I were a man, I'd. . . ." But, of course, this sentence must remain incomplete.

We have to admit, up front, that men do not have an easy life either. They, too, suffer from injustices, uncertainties, and confusions. They are driven by a different set of devils; many are a result of the confusion in women's lives. While we are focusing on our own plight, we must always bear in mind that those of the male gender definitely have their share of complaints. It's important to retain a sense of perspective and understanding for "the other side of the coin" if we are ever to make any progress ourselves.

But once we have acknowledged that men have problems, too, we are left with the question central to *us*: "How'd we get into such a mess?" What did we do to deserve the pressure of two different roles? Why are we so confused when our grandmothers, whose lives were frequently hard, were nonetheless clear about their role?

These questions have plagued me for years. I'd read anything and everything I could to gain a sense of women's history. During my college years, I'd turn any term paper, in nearly any class, into a self-search project. I still remember one professor's comment: "So what does women's rights have to do with Neanderthal man?"

Like most women, I've mellowed a lot since my idealistic youth. Much of the anger is gone; I tend to be more reasonable now, although I still burn, both inside and out, when I witness an open case of prejudice against women. ("We had a woman once, and she didn't work out; we don't want another one!") This mellowing has combined comfortably with the ability to see situations from more than one perspective. I no longer believe women have been oppressed for centuries as the result of some grandiose male conspiracy. No such organized effort could have worked so efficiently. Why it turned out the way it has, with women in a position subordinate to men, is not as important to me as how it all began to change.

HOW DID WE GET HERE?

In a free-enterprise environment, professional careers are highly competitive. It's the "civilized" rendition of the dog-eat-dog laws of nature. The best will survive, and we always hope the truly best ones will end up on top even if they play by the rules.

To be the best, a competitor must begin with the basic talents, but then he (and it usually has been "he") must develop those talents to the fullest. "Talent" includes the personality and charisma to work one's way through people coupled with knowledge and skill in a particular field. Even when these talents are all neatly integrated, the person must still be lucky!

Luck aside, those who are *highly* successful in their careers are usually those who give themselves totally to their work. One who has all the natural abilities and gives a 100 percent effort is generally a better bet than one who has all the natural abilities and gives only a 75 percent effort. Some companies have demanded this total commitment from their employees, logically assuming that this was the way to stay ahead of the competition. Many men have been married to their careers, and many have received some measure of career success as a result of this dedication (their neglected family life being considered an irrelevant issue by their employers). Some young trainees have reportedly been told, "If we had wanted you to have a wife and family, we would have issued you one!" Other companies have not been so blatant about their real demands. Efforts to minimize their employees' family lives have been more subtle, although some have developed elaborate, patronizing methods to keep the "little woman" in a nonbothersome place.

The "little woman" has nevertheless been a real help to many warriors of the business world. Many companies have lucked out by getting two heads for the price of one when the male employee came equipped with a supportive, loving wife. "The wife" soothed his weary brow, prepared his food and clothes, satisfied his sexual and emotional needs, and took care of "his" children. Additionally, she frequently acted as a sounding board for all the frustrations "her man" built up on the job. Many women also quietly took the verbal and physical abuse generated by a competitive work situation. Some women realized their men had to let off steam some-where; others cried silently, wondering what they had done wrong.

"The wife" was the extraspecial plus that gave those fighting their way to the top the edge. If a man was extremely lucky, his wife was also a psychological motivator, combining an encouraging nature with gentle love and soothing words. This winning combination was certain to put him on top!

Of course, the successful male professional was the one to bask in power and glory. He had the ability to make money, and money was the way everyone kept score. Some will point out that most men shared their financial rewards with their wives, but their sharing wasn't really all that magnanimous. Many of these men carefully guarded their earnings, as-signing household money to their wives. (It's called an allowance if you're a child.) Besides, it was only money. The true prize was the power, the accomplishment. And that was all his! She could glean a little glory by letting it be known that she was attached—as his "Mrs."

As long as one sex was the helped and one sex was the helper, the system worked well. There was a balanced organizational structure despite some glaring faults too involved to review here. It was a stable system; people knew their place.

Then one day the helpmate rebelled and wanted out of the subservient role. That movement caused nothing less than a total social revolution, one that will take generations to resolve.

THE MOVEMENT BEGINS

The women's liberation movement was inevitable in this country for at least two important reasons:

1. Our society is theoretically based on the belief in freedom and equality for all.
2. Our economic success laid the groundwork for the entrance of women into the mainstream of business life.

The genesis of the women's movement began with the freedom move-ment for black Americans. Its spark was a lawyer's daughter, Elizabeth Cady Stanton. Stanton's sense of justice was sharpened during the years she played in her father's law office. Judge Daniel Cady spent hours listen-ing to the complaints of many clients, but the ones he was unable to help were usually women. The tears of these women impressed young Eliza-beth, but it was the death of her brother, her father's pride and joy, that provided the impetus for her resolve to break out of her destined role.

Beside her brother's deathbed (her biography reports), Elizabeth climbed up on her father's knee to console him. His sorrowful sigh was followed by the words, "Oh, my daughter, I wish you were a boy!" Elizabeth met the challenge by stating, "Father, I will try to be all that my brother was."*

Elizabeth Cady eventually married Henry B. Stanton and became the mother of seven children. She was not eager to marry and had broken her engagement once. She changed her mind, however, when Stanton decided to attend the World Antislavery Convention in London in 1840. At this convention, she and Lucretia Mott were among the women who were ordered to sit in balcony seats during the proceedings. It was also at this convention that she began to realize the difference between equality in theory and equality in practice.

Back in America, continual pregnancies kept her from the intellectual activities she had grown to enjoy. Her dissatisfaction with the life of a woman grew. She wrote:

> Up to this time life had glided by with comparative ease, but now the real struggle was upon me. My duties were too numerous and varied, and none sufficiently exhilarating or intellectual to bring into play my higher faculties. I suffered with mental hunger, which, like an empty stomach, is very depressing. Cleanliness, order, the love of the beautiful and artistic, all faded away in the struggle to accomplish what was absolutely necessary from hour to hour. Now I understood, as I never had before, how women could sit down and rest in the midst of general disorder.
>
> I now fully understood the practical difficulties most women had to contend with in the isolated household. Emerson says, "A healthy discontent is the first step to progress." The general discontent I felt with woman's portion as wife, mother, housekeeper, physical and spiritual guide, the chaotic conditions into which everything fell without her constant supervision and the wearied, anxious look of the majority of women, impressed me with a strong feeling that some active measures should be taken to remedy the wrongs of society in general and of women in particular.*

Elizabeth Stanton's "remedy" became the first Women's Rights Convention. It was held in Seneca Falls, New York, in July 1848. It was organized because Stanton and a number of other women had a general feeling of being wronged but didn't know what to do about the injustice. The newspapers that commented on the convention incorrectly identified its organizers as "sour old maids," "childless women," or "divorced wives." Why else could they be upset?

---

* Elizabeth Cady Stanton, *Eighty Years and More* (New York: Source Book Press, 1898), p. 1.
* Ibid., p. 148.

The Declaration of Sentiments, the document that came out of this convention, was a modification of the Declaration of Independence. It read, in part: "We hold these truths to be self-evident, that all men and women are created equal. . . . "

The convention delegates identified elective franchise as the tool that would bring equality to women. The vote became the focus of the women's movement for the next 72 years. It was not until 1920, with the passage of the nineteenth amendment, that women received the vote. (This was 50 years after black men received the vote with the passage of the fifteenth amendment in 1870.)

Unfortunately, franchise was not the final answer to the frustration of women. Too much hope had been placed in the vote, and much of the momentum of the women's movement dissipated once the right to vote was achieved. The passage of the eighteenth amendment (prohibition, the year before in 1919) also served to quiet and dissolve a powerful women's group; the Woman's Christian Temperance Union, which had united thousands of women in a common cause, all but dwindled away once its goal was achieved. The passage of these two amendments was an important event that slowed the women's movement. Prosperity following World War I called men and women alike to enjoy the luxuries available to them— and to forget about causes, particularly ones they thought were settled.

Of course, we can't blame (or give credit to?) Elizabeth Cady Stanton alone for the women's movement. There were many powerful women who worked with her and independent of her to bring equality and the vote to women. Susan B. Anthony, Lucy Stone, Charlotte Perkins Gilman, and Carrie Chapman Catt (who led the final push for the vote in the early part of this century) were just a few of the many women (and there were men as well) who worked to gain a sense of independence and individuality for women. These radicals, for they were radical at that time, were just the first of many leaders who charted the way toward a goal we've yet to achieve.

ECONOMIC "SUCCESS"

The economic success of America also served as an invitation for women into the mainstream of business life, but at first the invitation was for low-level jobs. The New England cotton mills offered work to the daughters of local farmers as early as 1820. Twenty years later, women made up nearly half of the employees in the seven largest woolen mills. These were generally poor women and unmarried women.

Later, many of the married women left employment as cheap labor as their husbands' salaries increased. The nonworking wife became a status symbol for men. Henry James noted that while the American man was making money with a "terrible dedication," his wife "has been sacrificing on the altar of the graces." Lord James Bryce also noted that "in a country where men are incessantly occupied at their business, the function of keeping up the level of culture devolves upon women."*

As late as 1880, fewer than one married woman out of 200 was working working outside the home. Although this number doubled in the next 20 years, the figure remained low, and by 1920, there was a decline in the number of married women working. The overwhelming majority of women therefore had no monetary input into meeting the needs of their families; and as the dollar gained in importance, the contribution made by the husband to the family unit became disproportionately important when compared with the wife's contribution.

A woman's direct responsibility for her children also began to decrease as schools began assuming many educational duties. Children often became a burden rather than an asset as legislation required them to spend their days in schools rather than in factories. (This law worked a particular hardship on people of the lower working class.) With the help of new birth control information, the size of the families themselves began to decrease.

Medical science had also improved to the point where life expectancy was increasing. Women had even more time to kill. With no financial obligations or power, and with decreasing child-related duties, a woman had little to do but be a "badge of honor," heralding her husband's financial triumphs.

Education added to the uneasiness of being a badge of honor. In Colonial days, elementary schools offered boys and girls the same basic education. There was violent disagreement over higher education for women, however. It was not until 1837 that Oberlin College opened its doors to women applicants. After the Civil War, other private colleges did the same.

Some women tried to define and identify their role in maintaining the family. Some argued that they were indeed a part of the economic process; after all, the family couldn't eat or wear the money their husbands brought home. Someone had to transform that money into food and clothing, and that someone was the wife. A few women felt men should pay their wives in recognition of their contribution to the family. It's interesting to note

* Page Smith, *Daughters of the Promised Land: Women in American History* (Boston: Little, Brown, 1970), p. 80.

that this suggestion was still being debated 100 years later. This idea is useless, however, for it still makes women economically dependent upon men.

THE CLUB MOVEMENT

With economic opportunity closed to them, many women began searching for other ways to gain an identity distinct from their husbands'. The increase in the number of hereditary associations during the latter part of the nineteenth and early twentieth century was a particular example of the desire of many women to add to their personal status. Property inheritance, of course, gave a woman monetary value for a prospective husband, although this worth was usually inherited from another man, her father.

For a larger number of women, symbolic inheritance was often seen as important. A good name and background could add to a woman's personal worth. A familial association with a person who came over on the Mayflower or a man who fought in the Revolutionary War became most important.

Hundreds of miscellaneous women's clubs sprang up across the country during the last part of the nineteenth century. The General Federation of Women's Clubs, uniting many smaller clubs from across the country, was organized in 1889.

Early writers have often used the phrase "all dressed up and no place to go" to describe many women of this period. These clubs gave the women something to do for themselves apart from their functions as wives and mothers. Most of these clubs had a humanitarian focus. They sought to establish world peace, rescue the downtrodden, support missions, and (as mentioned earlier) save humanity from the evils of alcohol. By the 1930s, however, many social services were transferred to municipal, state, and federal welfare agencies, thus depriving women of an extremely important and fulfilling (though unpaid) area of intelligent activity.

WOMEN IN WAR

Wars also provided women with activity that was both intellectual and important, with each war taking women further from their traditional role. War was, and is, an important issue to women because of its effect on the family. From the American Revolution on, American women have been involved in war. The first war, the one for independence from England, encouraged women to ask questions of government. The Civil War found even more women involved on the battlefields and in hospitals, and the Spanish-American War elaborated upon women's skills through the formation of a nursing corps and the activities of the American Red Cross.

World War I found women holding down jobs previously held by men. Women did well in these jobs, and the passage of the woman suffrage amendment in 1920 was due in part to the useful service of women in the war just concluded.

During World War II, 6.5 million women went to work. These women were told it was their patriotic duty to fill the jobs left by the soldiers. Rosie the Riveter became a national symbol, as woman met the industrial machine.

Apparently women enjoyed their wartime responsibilities. Surveys taken toward the end of the war reported that 75 percent to 90 percent of the female workers wanted to remain in their jobs after the war ended. There were some efforts to get the government to continue the operation of day-care centers and female employment during peacetime, because (at least some people felt) these women shouldn't be cast off when they weren't needed anymore.

These postwar suggestions were never implemented, however. Two months after the end of the war, 800,000 women had been fired from aircraft companies; by November 1946, more than 2 million women had been dismissed from their jobs. Most of them were out pounding the pavement, seeking new employment.* Of course, many of these women were eager to get their lives back to normal with their favorite returning soldier, but the numbers who wished to continue their careers are startling, nevertheless.

"Normal" was never the same again. The war and the postwar activities forever changed the relationship between males and females and the general structure of the way we live. GI Joe frequently found that the winsome sweetheart he left behind had become a responsible industrial worker during his absence. She had survived—and survived quite well—without his constant advice on every issue. Yes, she wanted to marry and have children, but never again could she return to being the dependent little girl she once was. Perhaps it took a war to do it, but she had extended herself and met the challenge. She had a taste of independence

* Mary P. Ryan, *Womanhood in America: From Colonial Times to the Present* (New York: Viewpoints, 1975), p. 318.

and decision making, and once a person has this intriguing sampling of calling the shots, she seldom chooses to go back. Indeed, perhaps there is no choice, for who can unlearn at will and return to the days of innocence? Experience, even when it's forced experience, inevitably involves growth. Once a woman proved to herself that she could handle positions she once thought were impossible for her, she lost her awe of others in those positions. Once a woman knew she could do the work of a man, it became difficult to respect a man simply because he was male, even though she might respect him as a person. She realized that a person's sex is no measure of ability. She became more discriminating and difficult to impress, even though part of her still wanted to be impressed.

OPPOSITION TO CHANGE

Once the idea of the natural superiority of males had been questioned, we were faced with strong forces demanding a return to the "way it used to be." This call came from two masses of people:

1. Men, of course, *liked* believing they were naturally superior. Most of them understandably resisted every claim to the contrary. Who can blame them? It's wonderful to be on top, particularly when you've generally had someone supporting you to make you feel good and important. Although some men have now come to realize that there are problems with the superior/inferior relationship with women and that there are benefits to be gained from treating women as equals, many men would just as soon keep their upper hand, their advantages.

2. Many women have never personally had the opportunity to prove to themselves that they, too, can *do it*. These women cling to their traditional roles, which are comfortable and nonthreatening. Many of these women secretly believe that a few women possess that special skill most men have but that they, personally, do not. It's difficult to convince these women that success is within them, if only they would decide to call upon it.

Women are also held in bondage by their feelings and insecurities. Insecurities are so much a part of the human condition that the idea of women working outside the home touches on many of them. A lot of men would rather have a woman on their team instead of a woman challenging them for the very position that was already difficult to win before so many women decided to throw in their hats. Competing with women is unfamiliar and threatening.

Many women question their own abilities so much that they don't want to take the chance of testing them. If they don't try, they can't fail. It's safer for them to let someone else guide and protect them. If a woman wasn't given a lot of self-confidence as a child (and positive self-images have not generally been associated with female childhood experiences), she's even less likely to believe she has inherent capabilities beyond her present level of achievement.

THE ROCK AND THE HARD PLACE

Yes, we seem to be caught between that fabled rock and a hard place. We are lodged somewhere between our dreams of challenging all our abilities and our memories of a sweeter time when our abilities didn't require challenging. Many of our men have been unhappy partners in our search to find satisfaction. They are now searching, too. Many heartaches and tears have developed inside us as we all seek a comfortable resolution.

Unfortunately, there is no comfortable resolution. There are no black-and-white answers to the difficult question raised here. There are only changing values, situations, and choices that are bound to leave us wanting in some area(s) of our lives. We must deal with the difficult problems that have resulted as women continue to try their wings—and find they much prefer flying! And while they fly, there are myriad problems back in the nest:

- Who does the housework women used to do?
- Who nurtures the husband and the children?
- Who nurtures the woman in her new role(s)?
- Who makes the final decisions when decision making is no longer exclusively a male domain?
- Who takes responsibility for other family members now that a woman's time is otherwise occupied?
- Which activities are really necessary for the functioning of the group, and which activities are only thought to be necessary because "it's the way it's always been done"?
- Who becomes the cement—holding things together for everyone?

The situation today is even more difficult than a lot of people realize. In many ways, we have progressed to the point where the laws reflect equality, while the social and psychological reality is that equality does not exist. Although a woman may have many superior skills and abilities, they aren't the ones that easily fit into a game devised by men. Many women in our generation are falling through the cracks of our present system. Millions are left with the negative fallout of the women's movement:

- They have children to raise without a husband and frequently without support money.
- They are losing their children to a husband who has the money to buy the lawyers to get the children away from his ex-wife.
- They have the right (and the *duty*) to compete in the job market, but without the needed skills or experience.
- They have the right to give themselves to a full-time job and then return home to face their other full-time job.
- They have the right to fight the overwhelming power of tradition, which dictates what "women's work" is, and try to get some help from their husbands and children or (if lucky) from paid employees.
- They have the opportunity to feel guilty most of the time, because women, too, are products of their culture and believe much of what they've been told—from both directions.
- Women are available to accept the anger of men and other women who are settled in different life-styles, resisting anything unusual or challenging to their traditions.
- They are free to long for a simple way to be happy and to have it all.

This book will do a lot of things, but it does not promise simplicity, happiness, or a magic key. One of the most important truths we must realize is that the name of the game is *choice* and *compromise*. Everyone must give up something in order to gain something else. If you have only 24 hours a day to spend (and that's all you do have), you cannot spend 40 hours a day, no matter how organized you are. You must always ask yourself, "What is this activity, this position, or this judgment costing me?" And you better believe it's costing something!

Economic progress, the separation of children from the home, war, and higher education have brought us to this impasse. Hopefully, we can now use our intellect to analyze the situation and plan rationally for a somewhat uncertain future.

We must go with what we know: The economy will not continue to expand at the rapid rates we saw in the forties, fifties, and early sixties. Our general standard of living has peaked; we are called upon to be more prudent than in the past. The schools are losing their dominance over our children; we are regaining more responsibility for the children as many schools are finding themselves on shaky financial ground. And, of course, war always looms as a very real threat.

The challenges of today's world call for all the power we can muster. Our nation can no longer afford for any woman to be "a badge of honor, heralding her husband's financial triumphs." In the words of one weary combatant, "We need all the help we can get!"

Let's begin our analysis with a careful look at woman's own worst enemy: herself.

3
WHEN YOU TAKE YOURSELF TO LUNCH, ENJOY THE COMPANY

HER OWN WORST ENEMY

"We has met the enemy, and she is us!"

Pogo's words of wisdom were never more true than when applied to women today. The problems any woman faces begin within herself. She is frequently her own worst enemy, no matter how much she likes to blame history, the weather, the economy, her flat chest, her boss, her mother, or her cousin Harriet's domineering ways. We are never so quick to "pass the buck" as when we're making excuses for our own failings.

To complicate matters, we measure our failings so quickly, so inaccurately, and so badly. There is no accepted definition of success or failure; thus, many of us judge ourselves negatively because of certain vague feelings or impressions.

People today seem to thrive on individuality, yet they suffer from it at the same time. In a very strange way, we can say it's "in" to be unique, because everyone's doing it! This uniqueness provides a richness of character that makes being a woman in the last half of the twentieth century so challenging.

Our differences are fascinating, for they grow from a combination of our innate characteristics and our environment. Think, for a moment, of the bizarre implications for conflict that arise from some basic differences among us:

Some women were raised in wealthy homes, and others were raised in poverty.

Some had loving parents, and others had no parents at all. Worse yet, some had parents who didn't care for them or mistreated them.

Some women have been given the gift of glowing health; others have been sick most of their lives. Some have the mental stamina that comes as a welcome byproduct of a strong body; others lack inner strength, no matter how physically strong they are.

Some women today have the kind of drive and ambition that faithfully pushes them toward a specific goal; others might like to have a goal, if only someone would hand them one.

Some are blessed with the gift of personal intelligence. Others were not so lucky and do the best they can. Some women are book-smart, while others have an uncanny knack for focusing on the crucial practical issues. Some women were fortunate enough to develop their natural intellect with varied experiences and good schooling; others were never challenged beyond what was minimally required.

Some women are assertive. Others internalize their personal disappointments until they destroy their belief in their own ability.

Some women have that special pizzazz that draws people and good luck to them like kids to lollipops at a Fourth of July parade. Others aren't so fortunate; nobody likes them.

Some women are blessed with the Western world's idea of physical beauty; the lucky ones know how to carry it off. Others were obviously dealt a raw deal. On the other hand, some women can turn the loveliest face into a perpetual "before" picture, while others who don't happen to have perfect cheekbones and haunting eyes manage to be beautiful anyway.

Some women have a good sense of time; they make it work for them and seem to have more of it than other people. Others never know what time it is; they're constantly frazzled and rushed.

Some women handle stress well. Others fall apart at the sight of a broken fingernail.

Some women gain strength and peace from their belief in a Greater Being; others put their faith and trust in no one at all.

Most of us aren't permanently at any of these extremes. We fluctuate. Some days we're relaxed; other days we're juggling 29 crises a minute. Some days we're confident and positive; other days we're dejected and negative. Some days we feel beautiful and capable; other days we know we're the ugliest creature on two legs and can't do a thing. Although some of this ambivalence slows down as we age, many of us are hard put to say exactly who we are from day to day. No wonder there isn't now, and never can be, a "perfect 10" to use as a measure. We are each left to judge ourselves, against standards we have chosen personally. We should choose our standards carefully; our choice makes more difference to us than it does to anyone else.

THE SEVEREST JUDGE

Most women don't need an outside critic to tell them they're doing it all wrong. They tell themselves daily that they're making a mess of things.

Ann Nelson,* a 31-year-old sales representative for a major firm in Illinois, admits she's a problem for herself. Ann states, "I wish I had more time with my daughter, but then the time we do spend is harried. I'm always too distracted to make it worthwhile. I'm simply unable to relax. I feel there is always something that needs to be done! I can't just sit down or go for a ride on a bike."

Connie Pantelli, a twice-divorced mother of two who works as an administrative assistant in Columbus, Ohio, reports: "The time I spend with my children is filled with ambivalence. There isn't enough time for kids, plus me, let alone any kind of relationship! Then there's the guilt I feel when I wonder if I'm selfish for feeling the way I do."

And Barb Olson, another sales rep from Chicago, feels she has "terrible bad habits. I allow too much of myself to be 'all things to all people.' I allow things to pile up, and then they become overwhelming. I also spend too much time on the telephone procrastinating."

Like Barb, many women try to be "all things to all people"—and all things to themselves. When they do this, they set themselves up for failure. They're bound to feel inferior, for there is no way they can meet the demands they've imposed. They forget that everyone is inferior in some things—and it's healthy to realize it! No matter how many "how to" books you end up reading, there are some things you just won't be able to do.

This isn't to say we should stop short of achieving our greatest potential. We should strive for our personal heights. But there's a difference between having a realistic idea of your potential and shooting for a perfect score in 150 events! You are bound to be inferior at some things; a smart woman knows her weaknesses. She refuses to make herself feel inferior by setting her personal standards beyond her reach.

THE DIFFERENCE BETWEEN THE REAL AND THE PERCEIVED

Many women make life difficult for themselves when their perceptions of a situation differ vastly from the reality. These women believe something

* Although all situations described in this book are factual, all names are pseudonyms. In some cases, the name of the woman's hometown has also been changed.

is true, or something is required from them by others, when it really is not. For example, many women *think* they know what their husbands expect of them, when the truth is they know nothing of the sort. Frequently women think their husband believes the same things he believed 20 years earlier; they fail to note the changes that have taken place through the years. Also, many women blame their husbands for some of their own actions when the husbands had nothing to do with those actions. It was their personal demand for perfection and not their husbands'. Household cleanliness is a common example of this. Many women will scrub their fingers to the bone because "My husband likes the place spotless!" When questioned, many of these husbands report they seldom notice the condition of the house unless it is in a *total* state of upheaval! On the job, what a woman thinks is important to her boss is frequently unimportant, and how she thinks she spends her time is usually at variance with the way she actually spends it by 40 percent to 50 percent.

The difference between reality and perception is crucial, because a woman makes important choices about her life based on what she *thinks*. What a tragedy it is to spend a large slice of your life in a certain—frequently undesirable—way because you thought something was true but it wasn't! By the time you suddenly realize your mistake (if ever you do), you could have accumulated years of "misplaced" living!

How do you avoid this pitfall? Talk to people. Communicate. Search for the facts. If you want to know what your husband thinks, take the first step and ask him. Then, if you think he's playing games with you, ask again. Try to pinpoint exactly where he stands.

Do the same thing with your boss concerning your job. Does he or she really demand that you stay until 6:30 each night to do the job well, or do you only think your boss thinks you're dedicated when you do?

Do you believe the only way your kids will know you love them is if you carefully iron and fold their underwear before putting it in their drawer? Ask them and see. Better still, question some of your adult friends who talk openly about their loving parents. What was it in their childhoods that let them know their parents loved them?

And if you want to know how you really spend your time, keep track of it. Don't wait until noon or 6:00 P.M. to recall what you did on a certain day; record your "time log" every 15 minutes. After a week or two of keeping an accurate time log, you're guaranteed surprises. You'll say such things as, "I didn't know I spent so much time watching television," or, "I certainly put in a lot of hours doing those weekly reports—many more hours than I thought."

Perhaps a log on your time is the best way to prove my point about the difference between perceptions and reality. Time can be quantified, and when the figures are totaled, we can see how wrong we can be. Human relationship issues are not always as easily identified, yet they can be just as significant. Once you begin dealing with the realities of your life instead of with the way things seem to be, you will be closer to leading a life that makes you happy while making those around you happy as well.

MOVING FROM COMPLAINTS TO ACTION

Time—the lack of it, that is—is the subject of many conversations between working women. "There aren't enough hours in a day!" is a frequent cry in the subways, over the egg salad lunch, and in the powder room.

Donna Quinlan is a good example of a woman who seems to be "running double time" both at home and at the office. Donna is a 26-year-old administrative assistant for a credit union in Michigan. She has a year-old son and writes of her routine: "My husband starts work at 5:00 A.M., so by the time I get home from work, cook dinner, feed the baby, and clean up, he and the baby are ready for bed. Then I try to get my housecleaning done and still have time to do my hobbies or just sit and relax. This causes other problems, as I become uptight at not being able to do everything."

Donna doesn't seem to have enough time at work, either: "I never have enough time to finish a started project. I do work for three men who all seem to want 'rush' jobs completed at the same time."

Farther south, in Kentucky, Elaine Rogers echoes many of Donna's complaints. Elaine is a computer operator with two sons, four and ten years old. She writes, "Until two weeks ago, I was working 50 to 70 hours a week. Then I decided it was time to slow down. I still don't have enough time with my boys and my husband as well. I need time for housecleaning chores and a few minutes just to sit and unwind." And although Elaine enjoys her work ("I love computers and the amazing things that can be done with them!"), she still finds many time constraints. "It's difficult to find time for all the reports and duties to be performed in a week's time. I constantly fight people's individual requests or demands that keep me from working on the important priorities."

Time. We all seem to need more of it. And yet we have all the time there is. We can't borrow any of it from our neighbors (as grandmother used to borrow sugar), and we can't save the few hours that accidentally become free on Monday for the Friday that is always hectic. All we can really do is *spend* time.

It will surprise no one to learn that some of the biggest time problems are reported by women with young children and outside jobs as well. It's also not surprising that the more young children a working woman has, the more pressing the demands on her time. It appears that, as children move into their teens and twenties, there are many new concerns, but there is some relief from the daily hassle of mom doing it all. For many women, however, new time problems develop that replace the old ones.

Getting control of your time is the key to getting organized. Time control means getting the most out of your day, realizing you won't be able to do everything. It means making the best use of the time you have available, doing what you can with it, and accepting the fact that you have done a good job and can do no more. A number of women wrote me saying they live by the popular serenity prayer: "God grant me the serenity to accept the things I cannot change, the courage to change those things I can, and the wisdom to know the difference."

Do you have the courage to change the things you can? This is not a question to be taken lightly. Many people will easily answer, "Of course, I'll change the things I can change! Everyone wants things to be the best they can be! It's just that most things are beyond my control; I can't do anything about them!"

A person with this attitude will seldom change a thing. She will continue to complain about the problems in her life, frequently enjoying her stories of woe. We all have known an "Aunt Verna" who makes a career of being unhappy. Nothing goes right in her life; if it did, she wouldn't have a thing to talk about. Her stories are her babies; her problems are dear friends; and she'd attack anyone ("I tried that once; it didn't work!") who'd dare to suggest otherwise!

How easy it is to see the problem when we smile knowingly at an eccentric old friend. After years of talking with her, we know she doesn't *really* want to change anything; she just wants to talk about it.

It's more difficult to see this tendency in ourselves. We, too, frequently pay a lot of lip service to solving our problems, but we really don't want change. Oh, we *believe* we want change, but we're only fooling ourselves. (The difference between perceptions and reality, once again!) We become so content with our old discontents that we'd actively defend our right to keep them rather than take a chance on something new and unknown. Most of us are afraid of change, and this fear has become an albatross around our necks. Our fears hold us back; they keep us from growing.

Do you *really* want control of your time? Do you want the surge of power that even the smallest measures of personal control can give you? Are you an "internal" person who truly believes you can make a difference, or are you an "external" person who would rather cast her fate to the winds? Are you eager to discover what improvements you can make before you accept the realities of those you cannot? If so, it's time to move ahead to the basic steps of time control.

BASIC TIME CONTROL

Time control begins with goals. If you've read anything at all in the past 20 years, you've seen the word *goals* at least 500 times. But have you ever applied it to yourself? Have you given the magic of goal setting a chance to work for you?

In one scene in Lewis Carroll's *Alice in Wonderland*, Alice is traveling through the woods when she sees the Cheshire Cat in a tree nearby. She asks the cat, "Would you tell me, please, which way I ought to go from here?"

The cat answers, "That depends a good deal on where you want to get to."

"I don't much care where—" says Alice.

"Then it doesn't matter which way you go," says the cat.

It's always easier to identify the problem when you're looking at someone else or, in this case, at a fairy tale. But apply the Cheshire Cat's pronouncement to yourself: If you don't know where you're going, any road will get you there!

Do you know where you're going? This week? This month? This year? In your lifetime?

If you have no goals, there is no such thing as a waste of time. If it doesn't matter to you or to anyone else what results you achieve, any use of your time is as good as any other use. Time will pass; it doesn't matter if you take a nap, read Shakespeare, write a report, or balance your checkbook. One activity is as good as any other.

When you have defined goals, however, there *is* a difference. One activity will move you closer to your desired accomplishment, while another activity will not. You are now able to make a judgment about your activity.

What exactly is a goal? "Aren't goals those things efficient people list each day?" you may ask. Or, "Are goals the same thing as dreams?"

My favorite definition of a goal comes straight out of *Webster's*: A goal is "an end that one strives to attain." When we speak of a goal, we are talking about that eventual end. An activity, on the other hand, is "a specific action" (again, according to *Webster's*). Specific activities are therefore the steps or actions you engage in to eventually achieve your goal. You hold a meeting, write a letter, or make a phone call (all activities) when your goal is communication. You purchase yogurt, broil fish, and make fruit salad (all activities) when your goal is a healthy family.

I make this distinction because many people run around in circles chasing certain activities they *think* are important goals. They generally end up running from activity to activity, pretending they're organized because they've put together some sort of list. They are usually wasting a great deal of time. Instead, they should ask themselves what is their objective and what activities will lead to it. When they do this, many options become instantly obvious that they have never thought of before.

Meetings are a wonderful example of this common disease, "activity-itis." Many companies have meetings just because "it's Tuesday, 10:00 A.M." Why? "Because we've always had a Tuesday meeting at 10:00 A.M." If pressed, this chief executive officer (CEO) would probably defend her routine by claiming, "important information is transmitted in those meetings!"

There's no question that important information should be transmitted. But what would happen if the CEO asked, "What is my goal?" Answer: "communication." Then if she asked, "What are my choices of ways to communicate?" Answer: "memo, phone calls, lunches, meetings, a bulletin, a morning letter. . . . " Some of these activities would be far more useful than automatically calling a meeting; most would save time; and each would get the job done. Of course, meetings are sometimes the best alternative, but the point is to distinguish between your *goals* and your *activities*. The difference between the terms is important, because they serve as a tool for clearer thinking.

GOAL GUIDELINES

Goal setting is not always as easy as we might think. How do you set good goals? The following are some simple guidelines for effective goal setting.

Goals Are More Powerful when They Are Your Own

As a family member, as a member of an organization, and as a member of society at large, we all have to be involved in activities that are not directly related to our personal goals and directions. This is part of the price we pay for being a member of a group, be that group a married couple, a political action group, or the global community. The individual "sacrifices" for the sake of the general good. Members of successful families must daily sacrifice part of their individual rights for the sake of the total family. Ideally, individual family members have united to determine family goals that are in agreement with each other. Even when this takes place, there are times when an individual member feels "put upon." (It's no news to anyone that many of us believe "the mother" in the family has been the frequent victim who has sacrificed too much for the sake of others.)

Once we have acknowledged that mature people readily make some personal sacrifices for the welfare of the group, we can return to the basic point here: Goals are more powerful when they are your own. Of course, one person can try to force another person to perform in a certain way against her will (particularly if the person doing the forcing is bigger than the person being forced), but her heart will not be in it. The goal will become merely an activity, done when the situation demands that it be done.

The best example of this is your 13 year old's bedroom. You can scream and holler until you get laryngitis for her to keep it clean. She'll do it— now and then—particularly if her allowance is based upon her doing it, but she won't do it "with love in her heart" (as my father used to say while he stood glaring in through my bedroom door). But then one day, the room is mysteriously clean. You wonder if she's ill. You ask, "What happened?" And she tells you, "I decided I wanted a clean room!"

Personal goals are dynamite. When a person finally realizes the real power inherent in making a crucial decision about what she wants out of life, she will be amazed at the things that can happen. As a well-traveled, elegant "grand dame of a lady" friend of mine once said to me years ago: "Be careful when you decide what you want, my dear. You may get it!"

Goals Should Be Written

There is magic in writing something down. Forming the words with a pencil or pen in your hand requires an act of commitment on your part. You have declared your intentions to the world, in a sense. The act of writing also requires that you think through your goals carefully enough to choose the proper words to express yourself.

When you "keep your goals in your head," you are not forced to be precise. Your goals can float aimlessly in your cerebrum for years and never go anywhere. There are observable clues when this is happening to you: You find yourself saying frequently, "One of these days I'm going to. . . . " or "As soon as winter's over I plan to. . . . " or the classic "Just as soon as things cool down around here I'm going to. . . . "

Pin those thoughts down on paper. Be careful and precise. Once they're on paper, stick them on the wall where you will have to stare at them each morning.

Goals Should Be Realistic and Obtainable

It is most difficult to identify what is "realistic and obtainable" for yourself. There is actually a very fine line between the possible and the impossible. You want goals that make you stretch yourself to your grandest heights; on the other hand, you don't want to set your goals beyond your personal reach, or you're doomed to failure. Once again, we must strive to decipher the distinction between what we *really* can do and what we *think* we might be able to do.

Personally, if I had to err in one direction or another, I'd push myself a little beyond. I say this with caution, because I know there are many women who have nervous breakdowns from trying to achieve more than their abilities allow. I've had some close calls myself. I feel this approach is O.K. for me, however, because I've worked to know myself since I was very young; I can handle failure fairly well now, and I know when to stop trying. But I've also achieved things beyond my wildest dreams and, through this approach, have found endless joys from knowing I can do it! There's exhilaration, my friends, in attacking your fears and pushing out those limits that you, and no one else, have set before you. Once you've learned you have more power and ability than you thought you had, you're anxious to dig even deeper to see what *else* you can do. It's such a game, and so much fun! All you have to do is give yourself permission to be free!

I still say, "Be realistic about your goals." I think it's good advice. But as soon as I suggest forming realistic goals, a picture flashes through my mind—a picture that appeared in a news magazine a few years ago. In the picture, a woman I'll call Carol Miller was grinning from ear to ear. Seventy-two-year-old Carol had something to smile about, indeed. A few years earlier, Carol had decided that her goal was to climb mountains. The only problem was she had never climbed a mountain before in her life. "Mountain climbing is not a realistic goal," her friends had warned. But Carol decided to climb mountains anyway, and she was in the news because of what she had done—climbed Mt. Everest! Yes, there she was in all her glory, backpack and everything, holding her victory flag up toward the clear blue sky! She had blown 'em all away!

You decide, as only you can: What is realistic for you?

Goals Should Be Specific and Measurable

Powerful goals become workable when you get a handle on them. Too many people make the mistake of developing loosely defined goals (I call them mushy goals). They will say such things as, "I want to be useful to others," or "I want to be a loving person." This fuzziness leaves you with the problem of never really knowing when you've achieved your goal. How do you know when you've arrived or even whether you're really moving in the right direction?

"Specific and measurable" means this: Instead of saying, "my goal is to be rich," write "I will have $5 million [that's definitely rich to me!] by July 1, 1990." "Five million dollars" is quite specific and measurable; either you have it by July 1, 1990, or you don't.

Goals Should Have a Time Schedule

You don't achieve your goals all at once. You move on them slowly, step by step. Ideally, your short-term goals (also known as "subgoals") and your long-term goals are interlocking—that is, they fit together, with the short-term goals building year by year, eventually leading to the successful accomplishment of your long-term goal. A long-term goal can refer to your five-year plan or to your lifetime plan. It is generally thought to involve a time frame longer than two years.

Both the long-term goal and the subgoals should have a timetable attached to them. Using the example of the $5 million, you might plan to make your first million by July 1, 1986; your second million by July 1, 1988; and so on. Then all you have left to do is figure out which activities will allow you to achieve these goals by the specific dates. "Slow but steady wins the race," and with proper goal planning and a little luck, you're sure to be a winner.

Goals Should Be Compatible

If your goals aren't compatible, you run into an obvious problem: The successful accomplishment of one goal will prevent you from accomplishing another. Getting your various goals to be compatible is not always an easy task. There are many women who will swear that having a successful family life is incompatible with having a successful career. Most of us would acknowledge that it's not a piece of cake. However, careful planning and a serious effort to see things as they are instead of as they appear to be allows us to maximize our chances for success while we minimize our chances for failure. It's important to approach conflicting goals with a level head, doing what we can to take the sting out of the conflict.

Many people are afraid of goals. They believe setting goals takes away the freedom from their life; many will say they'd rather live spontaneously. These fears are unfounded for at least two reasons.

First of all, your goals aren't carved in granite. As your situations change, your goals may change. As you grow and develop, different things will have greater or lesser importance. Your goals will reflect your changing values, experiences, and aspirations. But if you do not set goals, you are likely to find yourself buffeted about by all kinds of outside pressures, going first in one direction, then in another.

Secondly, personal goal setting is not an inhibiting exercise; it's a freeing one. People who react negatively to the idea of personal goal setting have the wrong impression of what it's all about. They think of the rules and regulations they used to rebel against when they were kids or teenagers; they think of goals in terms of "can't." Such thinking is negative—and needlessly so.

The act of goal setting is a liberating step. Instead of constantly running around in circles, you are now ready to move in a direction important to *you*! Goal setting is a *tool* for your use, much like a car; it gets you where you want to go. You still have the freedom of choice when you set goals, but with goals you know when you're making progress on what you want and when you're "taking five." Of course, there are always unforeseen events that shape your destiny. But when you are a goal-oriented person, you will be ready to accept events as they happen and move ahead with the new circumstances that have come your way. When you're given a lemon, you will have the skills to make lemonade.

SETTING GOALS

Once you understand the guidelines for setting goals, you are ready to get down to business; you are ready to actually begin setting goals for your life. Goal setting can be an unsettling, searching process, but it can also be a light and easy activity, especially at first.

Of course, you have but one life, and all the events in it are intertwined. For the purposes of easy goal setting, however, we can divide life into different aspects. These aspects of life will help you focus on the various roles many of us enjoy. While focusing on each aspect, let your mind run free. Don't be inhibited by what you think may be a problem. There will be time to sort out dreams from reality later.

Right now, turn your "someday dreams"—no matter how wild—into specific goals. Try to do this when you're insured peace and quiet, at least for 15 or 20 minutes. Hide away with a pen and a piece of paper and begin developing goals for the aspects of life discussed below.

Education and Personal Development Goals

Personal development is the process of our growing and becoming in this life. Of course, we learn daily by living, but frequently there are many topics that particularly interest us that we would enjoy if we took the time to learn more about them.

What subjects have you always wanted to explore? Was a degree program part of your ambition? Did you want to learn for fun? What skills have you always wanted to have? Have you cheated yourself by saying you're too old for them now?

Health and Physical Development Goals

Most of us have fairly good health and passable bodies with little effort—for the first 25 years of our lives. From then on, it's downhill all the way, unless we take some special care of the machinery. I, personally, saw such a change after 30 that I truly believed someone had switched me in the middle of the night and put me in an older body. It's amazing how the young believe they will always be young!

What level of health do you want? What are you willing to give and sacrifice to maintain this level of health? What special physical accomplishments would you like to achieve? It's never too late to do your best, and we do ourselves no favors when we claim, "You just get like this when you get old," or "It's what happens once you've had babies." It may be a little unrealistic to dream of having the body we wish we had had at 18 when we're past 40, but there's nothing wrong with having a darn good body for 40, 50, 60, 70, or 80! Our physical stamina affects everything else we do.

Spiritual Growth and Religious Goals

Much as our physical health affects everything we do, so does our spiritual health. In many ways, it's even more important. Our spiritual health defines the parameters for our evaluation of everything else. It provides the structure for our life, much as our skeleton provides the structure for our body. We can see our physical problems more readily, so it's easier to tell when something is wrong. It's not so simple with our spiritual selves: We can't physically touch the problem or stand before an X-ray machine. But the problems are real; we know something is particularly wrong when we can't seem to find peace of mind.

What are your spiritual goals? And your devotional goals? What are your goals for religious service?

Personal Relationships Goals

We do not stand alone; we are who we are in relation to those around us. We tend to get out of relationships what we are willing to put into them.

What are your goals concerning relationships with your spouse, parents, children, and other family members? What are your goals concerning relationships with your co-workers, your boss, and the friends you have in your various organizations and your neighborhood?

Career Ambition Goals

Some women are confused over why they are working. This confusion causes them a good deal of anxiety, since on one day they feel that putting in their time is enough, and on other days they chastise themselves for not being more competitive, more professionally ambitious. Ask yourself: What are my career ambitions? Why am I working? What do I hope to gain during my years of employment?

Status and Respect Goals

Although most of us want to be "respectable" people, different women have different needs for recognition of their work in their community. It is important to know, honestly, how much status and respect we need in order to be happy.

How much status do you need? What are your goals for community involvement? Whose respect is important to you?

Material Rewards and Possessions Goals

Some of us need more money than others. Some of us are more honest about how much money we need than others. We should at least be honest about this to ourselves.

How much money does it take to make you happy? What economic level do you aspire to achieve in your lifetime? What possessions do you hope to own?

Leisure Satisfaction Goals

Hobbies and sports add flavor to many lives. They put zing-power into everyday living.

How important are your hobbies to you? Which hobbies do you want to develop? What places in the world do you want to visit?

As stated earlier, setting these goals down on paper brings them just a little closer to realization. Our lives are a tapestry of happenings and events, woven together. We have a great deal of power to make that tapestry look the way we want it to look, if only we use the right threads—through active goal setting.

DEVELOPING PRIORITIES

A *very* long time ago, when I was a "sweet young thing" at Indiana University, I was dreamy-eyed over a handsome-hunk fraternity jock I'll call Hank. Many an important quiz, paper, and exam were sacrificed to the hours I spent daydreaming of love, all for Hank. I also spent a lot of time doing his laundry. Besides being a handsome hunk, Hank was very clever. To this day, he is the only man who ever convinced me to iron his shirts!

One afternoon Hank came over to my dorm to pick up the eight shirts he had left with me a few days earlier. I smiled proudly as I handed over his freshly pressed duds, but my smile turned to dismay as I heard what followed his brief thank-you.

"Donna," he said, "I like you a lot, but there are 20,000 girls on I.U.'s campus, and I only got so much time!"

Handsome Hunk Hank grabbed his shirts and walked out of my life. It was my introduction to being a C priority.

Like Hank, all of us "only got so much time." Most of us have more to do than we have time for; and, as we already know, even if we're organized, we can't do it all if there's more to do than time allows. We are forced to set priorities if we hope to accomplish anything at all. Unfortunately, setting priorities is often more difficult than arbitrarily crossing one coed off your list.

For working women, particularly those of childbearing and child-rearing age, the most difficult priority choices we have to make concern choosing between our career and our traditional homemaking responsibilities. (It's somewhat ironic, for as I write these words on a rainy Sunday afternoon, my five-year-old daughter, Jennifer, is running around the office I have at home, in the periphery of my attention. She's drawing pictures and tacking them on the wall, so that "when I'm not here, you won't be lonesome, mom." I know the conflict well.)

I believe there's a lot of game playing going on about this traditional woman/professional woman question. Many women have their gut telling them one thing and their intellect telling them another. Using their intellect, they surround themselves with friends who agree with their current opinion. These friends reinforce their ideas on the homemaker/career controversy, and they feel intellectually happy. They get nervous stomachs and ulcers, nevertheless.

The only way women can move beyond this ulcer stage is to begin analyzing their honest feelings about the two kinds of lives they want to live. Making one alternative more important than the other does not cancel the other alternative out; it simply gives you some sort of guideline for making your day-to-day choices.

Fifty years ago, we wouldn't have had so many choices. Our choice would have been made for us, and most of us would have easily moved into our roles as homemakers. A few women would have been uncomfortable, but most of us would have accepted this role rather easily. Today, while most of us would acknowledge that we have some responsibility to maintain and support our family, the question concerns how much responsibility—and how much less than our grandmothers had. The following quiz will help you answer this question.

THE TRADITION QUOTIENT QUIZ

The Tradition Quotient Quiz (TQQ) provides you an opportunity to measure yourself against the readily accepted role of women 50 years ago. In the TQQ, I have listed 50 tasks common to the traditional homemaker. In no way do I intend to pass a negative or positive value judgment on these tasks; I mean simply to list them so that you might have an opportunity to respond in writing to these tasks. Remember that the role of wife/mother today is in a state of drastic transition; no one can begin to write a job description for it in the 1980s. The best we can do is try to establish what it means in our own lives. After all, we have to live it, despite the difficulty of defining what it is.

In order to help you identify your feelings toward the traditional wife/mother role, respond to the 50 traditional duties shown on the Tradition Quotient Quiz. Respond on the basis of what you *believe*, not on the basis of what you do. To define the situation more precisely, assume that you have three healthy children, between the ages of 1 and 12, all living at home.

After you take the quiz on the basis of what you *believe* a woman's responsibilities are, it could be interesting—and dangerous—to take the quiz again, responding on the basis of what you *actually* do. You might learn more than you want to know from doing the quiz twice in this way. The two sets of quiz results may reveal a great difference between what you believe and what you really do—a difference that some women will find unsettling.

THE TRADITION QUOTIENT QUIZ

For each statement, indicate whether you think the task is never (0), rarely (1), sometimes (2), usually (3), or always (4) a wife/mother's responsibility. Don't try to overanalyze the questions; simply answer them straight out. This is not a competitive exam, and you'll never have to indicate your score on an employment application. It is meant only for you to use as a personal tool.

It is a woman's responsibility to:

Make the beds. _____
Clean the bathrooms. _____
Dust the furniture. _____
Pick up things. _____
Sweep or vacuum the floors. _____
Wash the windows. _____
Water the plants. _____
Prepare breakfast and lunch
  for family. _____
Prepare dinner for family. _____
Do the grocery shopping. _____
Set the table. _____
Clear the table. _____
Wash and put away dishes. _____
Bake cookies, cake, and
  bread. _____
Prepare guest meals. _____
Plan meals. _____
Change baby's diapers. _____
Read to children. _____
Play with children. _____
Take care of sick children. _____
Be with preschoolers full-
  time. _____
Discipline children. _____
Drive children to lessons and
  so on. _____
Settle arguments and smooth
  hurts. _____
Purchase clothes for family. _____
Make and/or mend clothes
  for self and family. _____
Launder children's clothes. _____
Launder husband's clothes. _____
Fold and put away family
  clothes. _____
Take clothes to cleaners. _____
           Subtotal _____

Attend school conferences. _____
Attend school programs. _____
Review report cards. _____
Volunteer for school proj-
  ects. _____
Work on religious commit-
  tees. _____
Encourage family to attend
  religious services. _____
Work with community ser-
  vice groups. _____
Write and send holiday
  cards. _____
Correspond with friends and
  family. _____
Plan and organize family par-
  ties. _____
Purchase presents. _____
Take care of aging parents. _____
Take care of household
  money. _____
Be understanding with hus-
  band; realize he's tired
  from work. _____
Prepare foods husband likes. _____
Try to be cheerful for hus-
  band. _____
Try to be interesting for hus-
  band. _____
Try to make children act
  right for husband. _____
Be ready to satisfy husband's
  sexual needs. _____
Set a positive tone for family
  living. _____
           Subtotal _____
           Subtotal left column _____
           TOTAL _____

Scoring

Once you have responded to each question on the quiz, you are ready to total your score. Add each column of numbers separately, and then add the two subtotals for your grand total score.

The higher your score (the highest possible score is 200), the more you tend to think like a traditional woman. When faced with tough choices, you would probably be happier in the long run if you chose the more traditional option (assuming you do have a choice in the matter).

The lower your score (the lowest possible score is 0), the greater your discomfort with the traditional role of women. When faced with difficult choices, you would probably be happier with the less traditional choice (if, in fact, you honestly have a choice).

Further notes: If you score less than 50, you are unlikely to be happy making choices that reflect the traditional role of women. If you score between 50 and 100, you *tend* to be a nontraditional woman, although the choices are not always clear-cut. If you score between 100 and 150, you *tend* to be traditionally oriented and would frequently be happier (given the need for compromise no matter what you do) if you made choices that were more traditional than nontraditional. And if you score between 150 and 200, you can safely assume that the traditional role of women would fit you well. This, of course, doesn't mean you can have the traditional role; for many women, this option is not available. It means only that you now know more about where you stand.

WRITING YOUR "ABCs"

Let's return now to the work at hand, setting priorities. To begin developing your priorities, go back to the specific goals you wrote for the aspects of life discussed earlier in this chapter. Next to each of your goal statements, note the importance of that goal to you according to the following scale:

A: This goal is very important to me.
B: This goal is moderately important to me.
C: This goal is not really too important to me.

After putting either an A, B, or C next to each goal statement, write each of your "A" goals on a separate piece of paper.

Now, the hard part: Read over each of your "A" goals and rank them according to their relative importance. Label the most important goal "1"; the second, "2"; and so forth, until you have ranked all "A" goals. When this task is finished, you will have a priority system for your goals.

A simple task? Of course not. But the alternative to doing it is even worse. The alternative is not knowing, always having a perpetual knot in your stomach caused by confusion and indecision. By forcing yourself to make some tough choices, you are handling a difficult situation to the best of your ability. You are meeting your life head on and making the best of what you have. You can ask no more of yourself.

TURNING GOALS INTO ACTIVITIES

Once you have carefully established your goals and determined your priorities, you are ready to get moving. You cannot, however, "do" a goal. Remember that goals must be divided into smaller subgoals. With subgoals, you can list the activities that will lead to subgoal (and eventually) goal success. For example, if you decided your goal was to "be hired as the director of sales in XYZ Corporation by July 1, 1990," what should you do tomorrow? If you develop a list of activities that will lead you to that directorship, you'll have a better idea about tomorrow. You might decide you need an MBA in marketing to achieve your goal. You can't get that degree tomorrow, but you can call a number of appropriate universities for an application for admission. The day after the first application arrives, you fill it out. When you have it completely filled out, you send it in, and so on—one step at a time. You build, activity upon activity. You may take detours now and then, but you move toward your goal, nevertheless.

SCHEDULING TIME

Your important-goal activity will have a tendency to get lost in the shuffle of a busy day if you fail to schedule your activities. Many a woman wastes time by trying, as she puts it, to "keep everything in my head." This works well if you have nothing to do. If you are busy and want to get something accomplished, write it down.

A daily "to-do" list is valuable at home, at work, everywhere. Most women find that it works best when they keep their to-do list for home separate from their to-do list for work. I have found that a combined list works best for me. I have modified my own favorite standard list to include space for:

Activities of other family members.
Personal activities for that day related to my long-term goals.

Professional activities for that day related to my long-term goals.
The phone calls I need to make.
The errands I have to run.
The vitamins I must take.
The exercise I plan to get.
What I weigh that day.
Any meals I'm planning to prepare.

On this written list you should indicate the time you plan to do each task as well as the priority you place on it. Scratching off miscellaneous items from the back of a grocery receipt is not as effective as using a regular format, suited to your needs. Once you have a workable format, consider the following points when scheduling your day:

1. When scheduling activities, never forget to keep your focus on the objectives you are trying to accomplish.

2. Schedule around key events and actions.

3. Pay most attention to scheduling early-day actions. If you plan to move on your most important activities early in the day, you gain momentum for the entire day.

4. Group related items and actions on the schedule. This saves energy as well as start-up and wind-down time.

5. Prepare tomorrow's schedule before you go home from work for the evening. At home, finish your schedule before you go to bed each night. Why? If you wait until the next morning, you've already got the day started. You'll end up planning—while the event is already happening.

6. Build in flexibility for the unexpected events. Since you know they'll happen, don't schedule things so back to back.

7. Include some thinking time for yourself. All of us need a private place to get our thoughts together. Where's yours?

8. Consider how to make waiting or travel time useful. Always carry good reading material with you. At least four times a week this reading material will save you from fuming because you're forced to wait.

9. Always put your schedule in writing. (Besides the points mentioned above favoring a written schedule, there's the point my wise old aunt use to make: "When you're past 30, three things happen to you. First, you lose your memory, and . . . I can't remember the other two!")

10. Control your unscheduled-action impulses. Use the list you make. Remember, your schedule is not dictating to you. You wrote it so you would have a guide for accomplishing what *you* want. When you find yourself tempted to engage in an unlisted activity, use your list as a curb: bump against it. Ask yourself, "Is what I'm considering doing more or less important than what I had determined was important for me to do today?"

If your answer is "Yes, it *is* more important," then go ahead and ignore your list. If, however, you realize you'd only be hurting yourself if you failed to follow your plans, stick to your list, accomplish your plans for the day, and stay on the road to success.

REVIEWING AND RENEWING

We all change, thank goodness, so the goals we write for ourselves when we are 20 will be inappropriate for the woman we've become at 30. (We should be most ashamed of ourselves if the goals we write at 60 are not *vastly* different from the goals we write at 20!) Sometimes the goals we set for ourselves at 44 are outdated by the time we reach 45. Because we change so much, and the people and events around us change us as well, it is important that we review our goals frequently and carefully as the years go by. The added advantage to this is that we can see the progress we are making as human beings. We can ask ourselves what we were thinking when we wrote the earlier goals and what has happened to us that has made us change. The interesting part of this exercise is that we never totally leave a goal; an old goal or an old dream is always a part of us, even if it's only a stepping-stone to another plateau.

Review your goals. What new insights into your life will now make an important difference to you? Where do you go from here?

Each day that we live is the mother to the next day. The days string together slowly, until all of a sudden, we have a lifetime behind us that seems to have gone by so very fast. The fascinating part of getting older is that our goals can become clearer and more complex at the same time. We can relax a little as we get more determined. We can challenge people more as we love them more. And we can forgive ourselves more often as we constantly push ourselves to grander heights.

Each day is renewal; yet each day is a foundation and a step. You are writing the story of your life every day that you live. How do you want the final chapter to read?

GETTING CONTROL OF YOUR BODY AND YOUR HEALTH

Many of us do not handle the pressures of our lives very well. We maintain an ideal in our minds and constantly measure ourselves against it. The result of the comparison is frequently negative. Often our lives do not seem to measure up to our ideal, no matter what we do.

Of course, this negative comparison does not happen only to women.

Men, too, suffer many of the same pressures and frequently feel life has handed them a raw deal. When these feelings of inadequacy grow to a certain point, we usually explode, in one form or another.

Liquor, drugs, and cigars/cigarettes have been used by people with all kinds of problems since the world began. People who use these products believe that they relieve tension, take the edge off, or make it a little easier. Some women, living at-home lives, have used these crutches to help them cope with their dissatisfactions, but today more and more women are turning to these aids to help them with the larger problems that have resulted from living two lives instead of one. Needless to say, women have no reason to be pleased with the statistics that show we are gaining an equality with men in their addiction to these killers.

Another health issue I believe is important—particularly to women— is fat. We all know many women who spend far too much time worrying about their weight. It is a major topic of conversation, tears, and anxiety everywhere you look. I have spent my life fighting this problem and am as tired of it as the next woman. I am, frankly, sick of it.

Unfortunately, there are no little skinny pills or simple answers to this problem, so my ideas will not be for everyone. I include some thoughts on the issue simply to provide possible insights for other women who also let their concern over weight get the best of them. Consider my thoughts, add your own, look over others' thoughts, and come to some conclusions. Define a workable weight-attitude goal for yourself. Plan for it and stop worrying about it.

For many of us, food is a way to fight back at the traditional role of women. The less we look like Miss America, the more we become our own woman. Of course, this is not a conscious thought. All the time we unknowingly feel like this we are jumping from diet to diet, trying to finally solve our weight problem. Our real problem is that we have conflicting desires, with the stronger, less logical desire coming out ahead.

Size has always meant power. "The bigger the better" has long been an unwritten rule of the jungle and the business world. Many small men have developed a "Napoleon complex" as a reaction to their size.

When you have meat on your bones, you have more mass. You feel as though you have more power and can't be swayed as easily. If men are not distracted by your vulnerability and beauty, they are more likely to hear what you are saying, although many of them might be threatened by their lack of power over you. In one sense, other women can relax a little more, too, when you're somewhat less than physically perfect; you're not as threatening to them, particularly if they are still into the feminine game. On the other hand, they, too, can be unnerved in the presence of a woman who feels powerful.

Many women have misperceptions about their size. It's almost as though they can't see in the mirror. Many who are extremely overweight see themselves as pleasantly plump when they look in the mirror; thousands of other women who are only five or ten pounds above their ideal weight see and think of themselves as fat. This negative evaluation of themselves can keep them in prison for years as they refuse to utilize their potential until they lose their extra weight. And of course, those unfortunate women who are starving themselves to death, suffering from anorexia nervosa, can't see themselves at all. They, too, are victims of the fat game; they are just currently playing by different rules.

I am happy to report I have finally made some progress in sorting this all out. I don't truly believe that after all these years I am ever going to be one of those women who is ambivalent about a hot fudge sundae, but I do seem to have found some guidelines that work for me. Perhaps you, too, may find them useful.

A Fat-Freedom Formula

1. Stop thinking of yourself as a weak-willed person who, if you were stronger, would happily stay on an 800-calorie diet and soon be at your ideal weight. Learn to relax with yourself more and to enjoy life today, whether you're at a perfect weight or a not-so-perfect weight.

2. Try to standardize your eating habits. *Habits* is the key word here, for habits are the key to food control as well as to control in other areas of your life. So if it is your habit to start the day with bacon, toast, and fried eggs; followed by hamburger, fries, and a shake for lunch; and a big steak, potato, and piece of apple pie for dessert at dinner, you have *problems*, unless your metabolism is a lot faster than that of the rest of us.

On the other hand, you can develop habits and structures that are consistent with your body's needs. For many of us who lead relatively sedentary lives, this generally means very little food.

I have also found that drinking water can keep you honest. If you set two quarts of water out for yourself each morning and drink it continually throughout the day, your appetite tends to stay under control. Coffee does not do the same thing. Water, of course, is also good for you.

Finally, drinking a good, vitamin-rich, low-calorie diet food for one or two meals a day can be most helpful. If you must go out to eat (or *want* to go out to eat), try to go to a restaurant that has a variety of salads or a salad bar. I always carry specially packaged two-calorie salad dressing in my purse, too.

I have tried, many times, to develop the habit of eating three sensible, well-balanced meals a day. Three square meals daily is a good way to live.

However, my problem with this approach is that I'm forced to deal too much with food too many times. (It would be fine if all I had to do was eat it; fixing it is the problem.) If you, too, find preparing three square meals a formidable challenge, it may help to use the easy products, enhanced by one leisurely, well-balanced meal of vegetables, fruits, fish or chicken, and grains.

Of course, whatever diet works for you and your health is the one you should follow. The important point is habit, habit, habit, habit, habit! Our routine determines what we become.

3. Get involved in something that you really *love*. There is some project or activity for everyone, and if you can find yours, you will also find a big ally in fighting your foodaholism. You can almost forget to eat if you have something you find truly important to fill your time and mind. If you have nothing that's really important to you at the moment, return to the aspects of life list you made earlier in this chapter. Consider the goals you wrote there that used to be daydreams. What can you do today that will get you moving on them?

4. Plan to get some exercise daily. *Exercise* is a dirty word for many of us who are flunk-outs from TV exercise programs and the two-for-one specials at the health spas. I have finally made peace with one terrific exercise: walking. I actually like to walk. I used to try to walk first thing in the morning before I did anything else, and I still occasionally do this. I have found, however, that a midday walk has additional benefits. It gives me head-airing-time. It provides a break from the long sits in my office chair. It allows me private time, when I can be alone with my thoughts and reassess where I am going. I have also found that walking exercises every part of the body if you walk vigorously. This was a surprise to me. In the summer, I bike everywhere around town and feel fortunate that this is possible where I live. All of this doesn't take much time, and once you get into the *habit* of doing something like this, it's more than fun.

5. As you get older, you may find you are more interested in health than in losing weight for the sake of beauty. Life is more enjoyable when you are well-tuned and well-fed. In my own case, I have also finally admitted that all the cookies I made "for the kids" were really for me. The children get their hands on more than enough cookies, cakes, candies, and ice cream outside the home. I've learned to make mom the one they can count on for the basic stuff—the foods that are healthy.

6. A new source of strength—one that has nothing to do with physical size—is the power you can achieve by having energy! With the proper diet to fuel exercise and regular living activities, you'll discover you can go a lot farther than you did when you were much younger. Organizing your life also provides you with a source of energy and power. Having

proved some things to yourself, you will be pleased to finally be able to apply what you have learned. This is a pleasure that gives true strength, not an artificial strength built on "bulk."

Our physical lives are intricately interwoven with our mental, emotional, and spiritual lives. We cannot separate them, nor can we talk honestly about women's directions today without addressing the issue of health, food, diet, and energy. We place many demands upon ourselves, and we owe ourselves the favor of providing "good machinery" to meet all of these demands.

GETTING OUT OF YOURSELF

One of the most difficult lessons any woman can learn is to be a friend to herself. This point should be taken far more seriously than most people do. It has nothing to do with being selfish, self-centered, or ego-oriented. It does not suggest that you put yourself before everyone else, always thinking of your needs before the needs of others. It does not mean that you must walk around all day patting yourself on the back and saying, "Gee, aren't you terrific!" It means what it says: Be a friend.

Being a friend to yourself means getting *out* of yourself, as much as possible. Many of us are so serious about "número uno," so introspective, that we lose the ability to see ourselves objectively. We analyze ourselves to death. We drive ourselves crazy thinking about "Who am I?" "Where is the real me?" "What will truly make me happy?" We think about these issues to the point where we're afraid to act on anything for fear it will be the wrong move, there may be regrets, or we may hurt a little.

There's no denying it's difficult to get out of yourself. We know ourselves so intimately that objectivity seems quite impossible. But objectivity and concern about us is what we would want from a friend, and I believe we can be a friend, in this sense, to ourselves. We still have a value for other friends, but we have an additional ally when we have ourselves as a friend as well.

Perhaps this is why the sea, the mountains, or even a walk through a blooming forest in springtime can be so peaceful. When we compare ourselves to the miracles of nature, our personal problems look so small and insignificant by contrast that we begin to understand what "getting out of ourselves" means. For most of us, it means relief.

I was introduced to the idea of getting out of yourself when I was a very young girl. At the age of 20, after two years of college and developing plans to marry my high school boyfriend, I decided to push everything aside and hop a plane for Europe. While this might not seem unusual behavior for many people, it was very unusual for a small-town girl from rural Indiana who had only been across the state line once in her life! My father objected to my wanderlust but finally relented; I was soon on a plane to Luxembourg and an adventure that forever changed me.

The details of that trip could be the subject of another book. But suffice it to say that six months later, alone and wandering the rainy streets of an old German town, I was in the depths of despair. Looking back today, I realize a lot worse things could have been wrong in my life, but I certainly didn't know it then! All I could think of was how terrible my circumstances were, that my burdens were more than I could possibly bear!

I came to the corner of a rain-drenched cobblestone street and looked up. Across from me was an English-speaking church. I decided to go in and sit down, drawn more by the language I could understand than by any religious principles. I listened carefully to the sermon that evening.

"There was once a man," the minister began, "who thought he had more problems than anyone else in the world. He continually cried and complained to God about these problems, blaming the Almighty for being so cruel to him.

"One day, God took the man by the hand and led him to an enormous hillside. Looking over this hillside, the man saw thousands of crosses of all sizes and shapes. When the man asked what these crosses were, God explained that they symbolized the problems and pain endured by thousands of individuals; the largest crosses represented those people with the greatest pain, while the smallest crosses represented those who had the lightest cross to bear.

"Then God asked the man to choose the cross he would rather carry for the rest of his lifetime. It didn't take the man long to choose; he quickly moved toward the smallest cross he could find, happily indicating that he wanted that one.

"'So be it,' God replied as he walked away. The man reached over to pick up the tiny cross and found it was the one he had been carrying all along!"

I have thought of this story many times since then. We know our own problems and hurts so much better than we know anyone else's that it's easy to think we have more problems than anyone else. We lose our perspective. We crawl so far into ourselves that we lose the "light" of reality. We tend to believe everyone else has it made; little do we know the pain they may be carrying, no matter how they act before the outside world.

The lesson of "getting out of yourself" has become clearer through the years. During the past ten years, I have had many opportunities to speak and lecture before audiences ranging in size from 8 to 1,000. Public speaking, as you know, is one of the most difficult things in the world for most people. Before you go on stage or up to the platform, there's a tendency to review a list of *self-conscious* thoughts, and by this term, I mean *conscious of self*. You think, "Oh my, I'm going to make a fool of myself!" "They'll think I'm crazy!" "What if I don't know the answer to one of their questions?" "What if they think I look silly?" "What if I trip?" and so on. All of these self-defeating comments have one thing in common: They concentrate on the *self*.

After many torturous events, I occasionally found I was able to forget me, "the speaker of the night," and concentrate on the problems and concerns of my class or audience. I was confident of my material; it was just *me* I lacked confidence in, so once I was able to forget about *me*, I was fine. I would concentrate on the problems and concerns of others and try to help them with those problems. It was as simple—and as difficult—as that. Yes, it still is difficult at times, because you cannot always avoid the destructive self-conscious thoughts, but you can train yourself to think of others *most* of the time. Getting out of yourself is the trick, whether you're on a platform or at your job.

When you maintain an objectivity about yourself, you can also forgive yourself for being less than perfect. Perfectionism plagues millions of women and haunts them at home and at work. Many of these women will readily admit, "I guess I'm a perfectionist," acknowledging that they're doing it to themselves. The truth is they're so self-conscious that they can't stand to be less than absolutely perfect. What a burden this is! And it's a burden to live and work with as well. There are so many things to do, and perfection is useful only on a very few occasions.

Those of you who suffer from perfectionism would be smart to review the Pareto principle, also known as the 80/20 rule. The Pareto principle states that "the critical elements in any set usually constitute a minority of the elements." As the 80/20 rule, it means 80 percent of the value is accounted for by 20 percent of the items. For example, 80 percent of your sales usually come from 20 percent of your customers. (Eighty percent of your problems come from 20 percent of your customers, too.) Eighty percent of your effectiveness comes from 20 percent of the things you do.

Think about these percentages. If 20 percent of your activity accounts for 80 percent of the results you get (take my word for it—it does), then the remaining 80 percent of your activity accounts only for the additional 20 percent of the results that bring you to perfection. Do you have enough time to give the additional 80 percent effort to get the remaining 20 percent benefits? Only you can answer this question for yourself, but in most cases, the realistic answer is no! Maximize your skills; don't limit them. Perfectionism can be a very selfish and shortsighted approach.

Your consciousness of self also accounts for endless interpersonal conflicts and frustrations. How many hours do you spend worrying that someone was unfair to you, someone was short with you, someone doesn't like you, or someone was rude to you? So what if this is the case? What do you gain by dwelling on these issues? You are not helped personally, and the "guilty" party certainly doesn't suffer unless you plan to enjoy an elaborate revenge scheme. (Now that's really worthwhile!) At some point in your life, it's important to realize you're not so special. One-half of the people you deal with are going to dislike you—or be upset with, or be rude to, or disagree with, or irritate, or offend you—at least one-half of the time. Once you truly accept this, you can live with it. Quit the "poor me" trip. You are the sorry, comical figure for suffering over it. You're even sorrier for dishing it out.

Instead, do yourself a favor. Forgive people who stick it to you. Try to understand the hurts that make another hateful; defuse them instead of misusing your time and talents to fuel the fire. Everyone has hurts and frustrations that cause them to act in negative ways on certain days. Those women who can identify the hurts and needs of others and make them feel better about themselves find true peace within themselves. No, this doesn't mean you're a fool for letting people walk all over you. It means you're confident enough in yourself to realize that the actions of others don't detract a bit from your personal value.

Remember: The best way to "kill" your enemy is to make him or her your friend.

Finally, let laughter be your ally. Even the most depressing scenario will have some events worthy of a smile—if not today, then tomorrow. If you can get outside yourself, you can look at the person you are and admit the truth: "Say, lady, sometimes you're really funny."

Before we pass out blame for the problems in our lives, then, we must confront the person who is most responsible: me. We must say, "I am the one responsible for *this* life, not my husband, my kids, my parents, my boss, or my co-workers." It's so easy to blame someone else that many of us do it continually. We get nowhere. We go around in circles with our accusations. If we continue in this way, we will likely have the same complaints at 80 as we had at 20. We will find we have lived a life without growth.

On the other hand, if we squarely face the frequent differences between our perceived world and our real world, develop our goals and establish a plan for achieving them, work to make our body act for us instead of against us, and learn not to take ourselves too seriously, we may have a chance. We can move confidently forward, knowing we'll run into problems, but also knowing we can handle them. We can learn to crave change, instead of fearing it.

Once we have a handle on ourselves, we are ready to turn to our environment—the circumstances and people around us. With a gentle touch backed by determination, we can confidently say, "O.K., world. Let's see what I can do next!"

PART II
ON THE JOB FRONT

4

STEREOTYPED BEHAVIORS THAT GET IN YOUR WAY

OR

I've got to hang up now, Harriet; my boss just came in!

The woman on the job is still considered a new, strange creature. Although millions of women have entered the workforce during the last 25 years, attitudes toward and impressions about women are difficult to change. Society at large still considers the working woman an oddity, particularly outside the larger cities. The single working women in the professions have led the way in defining what the new working woman should be. These single women still have to fight many of the stereotypes that plague all women, but they have a less complicated life than those who are wives and mothers as well.

Not only does that home life take its toll because of the many obligations a woman has to her family, but it also wears a woman down because of the heavy psychological pressures. It's not that easy to switch from a wife/mother role to a professional role. Put simply, you need an adjustment period between the time you take off your apron and the time you put on your business jacket!

Women who are attempting to keep a foot in a female world while moving into a still male-dominated world have many traditional attitudes and behaviors to overcome. Their own attitudes and behaviors can cause enormous problems, as can the attitudes and behaviors of those around them. Since we are mothers forever, and wives and/or homemakers for as long as we choose to be, many of our emotional ties to our "traditional side" will remain. Many of these ties are good feelings, and we don't want to lose them. On the other hand, part of the problems women face on the job front revolve around the fact that many supervisors don't believe women are serious about their jobs. They sense that women aren't dedicated and frequently feel that all women are merely putting in their time, holding a spot until they can return to their "true" profession, in the home.

Why are you working?

It is important to define this for yourself. If you *are* working simply to put in time, you still owe your employer an honest day's work. If your career is something more, however, you want to be certain you *look* and *act* serious about your work as well as *feel* serious about it. In order to do this, you must be careful of the traditional behaviors and attitudes that get in your way. First of all, you must identify these tendencies carefully. Once they are identified, you should check your own behavior and attitudes to evaluate personal performance.

Our discussion of traditional behaviors and attitudes that get in your way on the job will be divided into three main sections: (1) Taking "Home" to Work; (2) Appearance: Say What You Mean; and (3) The Social Club at the Shop.

TAKING "HOME" TO WORK

You've heard of taking your office work home, but have you ever considered how many women take their "home" to the office? This habit is far more common than the filled-briefcase syndrome. Worst of all, many women don't even realize what they're doing. It seems almost natural for many women to sneak in home work while on the job—but it can be very harmful to their jobs as well as to the perception of female professionalism.

How do you keep from "taking your home to work"?

Children at Work

First of all, don't bring your children to work with you. There are a few very special instances in which you are able to bring your children with you, but in most situations, children do not belong at work. This seems obvious to a lot of you (particularly to those women who don't have small children), but many mothers find it a very desirable alternative and will try to get away with it, when possible. Most employers will stop the practice as soon as it starts, but the negative perception of this woman remains.

Some women have their children drop in after school to visit for a while. Although it's nice to touch base with them, this practice can also grate on the nerves of your employer or other employees. More and more people are openly stating that they don't like children, and your child's presence at the office will provide them with one more reason to complain and cause trouble.

Before you bring any children into your work situation, check with your supervisor. Also, if you own your own business and feel your children should be allowed in your place at any time, try to hire employees who will love your children's visits, too. Discuss this point before you hire a new employee. Many employees will not object to these visits, particularly if there is a relaxed, pleasant atmosphere around the office. If this is not the case, however, your children will become a point of contention between you and your employees, although you may not realize it. People are reluctant to come right out and say they don't appreciate the boss's kid's visits; they will point to other things, skirting the real issue. Then, too, many children immaturely act as though your business is their business. They throw their weight around as "the boss's son" or "the boss's daughter." Needless to say, this can rub even the most understanding employee the wrong way.

Guard against extended telephone conversations with your children as well. Checking in with your children during your break is one thing, but long, involved conversations are out of line. Touch base, give them reassurance and instructions after school, but save the heart-to-heart talks for later. Unfortunately, it's one of the prices we pay for working at 3:00 P.M.; we're not there when the children arrive home from school.

It's not only the mothers of growing children who abuse free access to the telephone. In fact, the telephone offenders are frequently older women with children living out of state. Of course, they could call them at night, but many prefer to use the business phones at the office. These women would never think of stealing outright, yet they will steal time from their employer and the price of the call as well without batting an eye. Many of them justify this practice by claiming they're "underpaid" or "work harder than the others, anyway." By the way, these are the same women who slip their personal mail through the office postage meters. The impression they present has repercussions far beyond "a simple phone call." It adds to the general perception of unprofessionalism—both for them and for other women.

An indirect way women bring their children and grandchildren to work is through the candy, fruit, raffle tickets, and other items they sell for their offspring at the office. Not only does this practice take time, but it puts co-workers on the spot to buy products most of them don't want.

These sales also cause friction, as everyone strives to remember who bought and who didn't the last time. Help your kids during your own time, if your children's schools must engage in this practice. Keep your efforts out of the office altogether. In fact, you would probably find a productivity increase would result from outlawing such sales altogether, if you have the power to make such a ruling.

Health Discussions

Secondly, many women take their home to work with them when they talk a lot about the health of their family members during working hours. Of course, the wife and mother has always been the person primarily responsible for the health of her family, but many women make this their full-time occupation—at the expense of their job.

A sick child is one of a working mother's greatest fears. Even when a woman has her life coordinated fairly smoothly, the guidelines all change when a child is ill. Who comforts the child? Who takes the child to the doctor? Who sits at the bedside and feeds her chicken soup? Who wipes his feverish brow?

A sick child is one of the most difficult issues. As a mother, I know the maternal need to be with an ailing offspring; as an employer, I know that getting the work done is essential to a successful office. How do you justify getting upset with someone who needs to be with a sick baby? Yet how many thousands of dollars and how much business can you stand to lose because a key employee is not there? Everyone is in a no-win situation.

Since a mother can't be two places at once, this problem may be with us as long as women have both children and jobs. The best we can make of such a difficult situation is to follow some commonsense guidelines:

1. Evaluate which parent can get time off from work more readily. Sometimes this will be the mother, and sometimes this will be the father. If you're lucky, your husband will see both the problems involved and his own obligation.

2. Share the duty roster with your husband. When possible, both parents should take some time away from their jobs to see their child back to health. Shared duties should apply to the middle-of-the-night chores as well.

3. Grandparents can also be a big help during illnesses. If you're lucky enough to have a convenient or willing mother or father who can help you out in tight spots, you're in luck.

4. Relatives or friends aren't as good as mom or dad, but they can help with a sick child. Stay-at-home women resent taking over the "rearing" duties of working mothers, but many are willing to help in true emergen-

cies. Be certain to do as much as possible on a regular basis to carry your share of parental responsibilities, so when you are really in a spot, the other mothers will be more likely to be willing to help.

Women also waste a great deal of time at work and harm their professionalism when they constantly chatter about general health issues. One of our older, unmarried secretaries once pointed out how frequently women talked about labor pains. (She was disturbed, of course, because she had nothing to say in such conversations!) I'm afraid this is frequently a justifiable complaint. Labor pains, childbirth, and menstrual cramps must be among the most frequently discussed issues in this country. Men do not seem to talk so freely about their private bodily functions, thus emphasizing the freedom with which women discuss such issues. Keep these stories to yourself. We all have a hormonal cycle that affects us one way or another; it's about as much news as northern snows in January. So keep it quiet. If you must, talk about it with your sister-in-law in your kitchen on Saturday morning!

Nonworking Friends

A third way many women bring their home into the office is through their continual contacts with their nonworking friends. Nonworking women can provide some very negative feelings about working women, raising unnecessary doubts and questions regarding something they know nothing about. There's a noticeable defensiveness in nonworking women; this defensiveness frequently comes across as offensiveness as they criticize you for leaving hearth and home so you can buy a bigger car and new clothes. These feelings can affect your entire approach to your job, causing you to produce below your capability. It's difficult to leave old friends, but you'd be better off if you found friends who also worked and loved their involvement in the outside world. You will soon find you invigorate each other and all end up doing better work.

As with the children at home, many women spend too much time on the telephone with their friends. Again, they justify these conversations as a "break because I work so hard," or "I only talk a few minutes, anyway." We've talked a lot about perception and reality in this book, and this is another case where the two are frequently far apart. The conversation that "only took 5 minutes" probably lasted 25 minutes. Again, the employer ends up paying and getting nothing in return.

The employer also pays when an employee "does jobs for the governor." In case you haven't heard this phrase before, "the governor" is your friends, family members, or you, yourself. "Government jobs" are tasks totally unrelated to the work at hand but done on company time, never-theless. Since many women have not discovered how to say no, they fre-quently find a way to sneak these other assignments into the work sched-ule. The standard justifications apply, once again; besides, who wants to pay to have it done? The office copier is frequently used for these jobs.

A "Homey" Environment

Finally, many women actually bring their "house" to work with them. Some bring mending and sewing projects, cookbooks, and repair jobs right into the office, planning to work on them at lunch hour. A lot of this work is done during extended coffee breaks that last far longer than orig-inally scheduled. The 15 minutes set aside for a cup of coffee become 45 minutes for sewing, chatter, and coffee as well.

Some women don't actually bring the work with them—just the ex-haustion. They get so involved in keeping the perfectly clean house they once kept (or their mothers kept) that they use up all the energy they have available. They "rest" at work, saving their energy for the next round of housekeeping.

Some women are also routinely late for work because of household obligations. They get in the habit of being 15 to 20 minutes late because they're getting things ready for dinner, dealing with the kids, stopping at the store, and so forth, on the way to work. Nothing is more unprofes-sional. Certainly, there are days when everyone is late; but when some women make a habit of this tardiness, it reflects negatively upon all women.

We cannot close the discussion of women who bring home to work with them without mentioning the woman who actually turns the office into a cozy little sitting room. Each office has its own personality, as does each occupant, but certain actions and arrangements are unsuitable for the majority of office environments.

I'm thinking of Shirley, an older woman who once worked for us. We knew she was a good typist because she had worked for us once before on a part-time basis, so we gladly hired her full-time when we found we had a need. She really didn't have to work, but her kids were grown, her husband worked, and she wanted something to do.

It happened gradually. First came the plants. The garden grew day by day. All the plants were healthy, and we agreed to install "grow lights" in dark spots. A few plants did enliven the office. All was well until there got to be so many green things that we had to duck to avoid them through the walkway and move them aside to see out the window.

Next came the coordinated decorations. We were surprised one morning to find matching pink and lavender curtains, file-cabinet covers (like runners on a library table), and cushions for the office chairs.

In this cozy little environment, Shirley typed now and then, but she also had a daylong tea party. At first, she carried a thermos, but eventually she brought a matching teapot and cup set. She'd sip quietly from her brew throughout the day. She complemented her liquid with cookies, apples, and cheese. This daylong munching, of course, left her lunch hours free, so she had the time to call her daughter in Louisiana during this period.

But the final touch was still to come: One wintry day she brought her hand-crocheted booties to keep her little toes warm! She looked very comfortable, even though she was frequently sick and kept us informed of her various ailments. Still, all in all, she looked sweet sitting there in her contrived little home, blowing her nose frequently on a delicately scented hankie. Her typewriter wasn't too offensive in this entire scene (it was fairly well hidden!). Besides, the mellow music from her portable radio covered the noisy clicks her typewriter occasionally made!

Why'd we keep her? Eventually, we didn't, but for a while it was fun to see just how far she'd go! Now it's a good story—and true! Shirley is a prime example of how unprofessional a woman can appear when she brings her home to work with her.

You're probably not like Shirley, but how much of *your* home follows you to work? Are you unconsciously defeating your goals to be and appear more professional by letting some of the points discussed here slip into your working day? Some work situations permit more leeway than others; that's why we allowed Shirley to get away with as much as we did. Remember this: Be aware of what you're doing and what that says about you. You may be one of your own worst enemies.

APPEARANCE: SAY WHAT YOU MEAN

Personal appearance has a far greater influence on what people think of us than we once believed. First impressions set the stage for all future interaction, and the way we look conveys the initial idea of who we are. Our dress continues to tell more about us than we may want known, so it is vitally important that we say what we mean.

"Pat" and "Patsy"

A few years ago, I had the pleasure of going to a five-day meeting of training directors in Chicago. Thousands of people were in attendance.

At the opening event, I mentally calculated that about 20 percent of the attendees were female. The meeting's format involved many two-hour sessions, which allowed the attendees to choose one of five sessions at any given time. One session immediately caught my eye: "Integrating Women into the World of Work."

This session drew an interesting group, but the ratio of men to women was the reverse of that at the conference in general. Over 80 percent of the group was female, which (not surprisingly) shows who's the most interested in women's issues! We talked about many things during that time, but the impressions of two women in particular are still with me.

Patsy was definitely "fluffy." Her makeup was vivid and artfully done. Her long, blonde hair cascaded around her bare shoulders. Her blouse was of the off-the-shoulders variety—white, with small eyelet lace as trim wherever trim was appropriate. The blouse was neatly tucked into an aqua-blue skirt, a billowing thing in full bloom, kept that way by several layers of crinoline undergarments. Her four-inch heels showed off well-curved ankles; pink toenails peeked out from the open end. She smiled all the time, and just like her long strand of pearls, her teeth tended to pick up the glare from the flourescent lights. She sat staring at Pat.

Pat wore a dark gray, pin-striped suit over a white shirt, buttoned to her neck. Her waist-long brown hair, undoubtedly left over from her college years, was clasped in the back, just above the collar of her suit. She wore no makeup; her steady dark eyes stared back at Patsy through thick, black-rimmed glasses.

Their eventual comments served only to confirm my initial impressions of them: Pat was always serious and intense, definitely against nonsense; Patsy was always giggling and silly, afraid of anything too involved. Pat was afraid her opinions on her job weren't taken seriously because she was a woman; Patsy never gave an honest opinion for fear someone would forget she was a woman. Pat was afraid sex would get in her way; Patsy had identified sex *as* her way. What did they have in common? It didn't take most of us long to figure out that they were both unhappy, confused, and insecure. Both had deep-seated fears and concerns over the woman-in-business role they had to define.

What does your appearance say about you? Does the way you look convey the impression you want people to have of you? Does it send messages that conflict with what you actually think and say? Can you dress for success without putting on a uniform and totally surrendering your femininity?

These are very difficult questions for many women. The ones who wear a uniform are lucky, in many ways, for the choice is made for them. Frequently, however, the uniform-wearers rebel, demanding the right to express their individuality. Women have been concerned about what to wear for generations; now our garments still confuse us, since what we wear reflects our continuing efforts to define our role. The traditional role versus our professional role remains an issue, even when we talk about something as superficial as the clothes on our back.

The Personal/Professional Balance

Of course, we all have our own style and preference, but how do you achieve that balance between your personal style and the unwritten dress guidelines for professional success?

The first step, of course, is to try to establish what those guidelines really are. Do you *think* no one really cares or notices—and they actually do? On the other hand, do you believe everyone judges your worth by the number of designer outfits you own? The fact may be that few notice, and many of those who do notice believe the need to wear labels indicates insecurity rather than style. (If you're confident of yourself, you don't have to put someone else's name on your behind or on your chest.) What's important, anyway, and what's not?

Clean is important. There's no disputing this. Even if you work in construction, you should start your day clean. Body odor, even when it's occasionally understandable, is difficult to overlook and creates a bad impression. Soiled clothes present the same image. The point about cleanliness may seem trite to many of you, but think again: How many times have you worked near an unclean person? In most cases, these people didn't realize they were offensive. Remember the old adage: "The fox can't smell her own den."

"The early morning rush" can cause us to organize a sloppy appearance for the rest of the day. Some of us have turned the morning routine into a regular game of beat-the-clock. With little attention to detail, we throw ourselves together, somewhat angry that we have to get up at all, but if we do, it's going to be as late as possible! We get so accustomed to hurrying and to the inevitable unforeseen events (such as a button's being off the blouse you had planned to wear, a run in your hose, and being out of gas) that we're actually surprised if we ever get to work on time.

The distant sister to those who race around each morning is the woman who wouldn't walk out the door without every cuticle, hair, and eyelash in place. I'm told there are more than a few who will rise from their warm beds as early as 4:00 A.M. to be at work by 9:00 (and they don't live a two-hour commute away from their jobs). "Why do you do this?" I incredulously asked such a woman once. "Why, I have to do my makeup, my hair, my nails, and my clothes!" was her indignant reply.

How much time do you need to give to the hair-nails-toenails-makeup game? Do you feel totally undressed if you haven't paid specific attention to each of these items each morning? Are you operating more from habit than from what you would choose to do today, if only you'd think about it? It's easy for all of us to carry our high school (yes, high school!) habits with us throughout our lives. Perhaps we try to look the way we looked at 17. There are now so many easy, carefree ways to approach our appearance that any time-pressed woman is foolish not to consider some alternative to her lengthy morning (and evening) routines. A lot of shortcuts involve hair care. Talk to your beautician for ideas and give yourself a break. Here are some quick appearance guidelines that work well for many women:

1. Start with simple. "Simple" means very basic, and any individual can build and elaborate nicely (when she has time and chooses to) from a simple base. Your appearance should enhance and complement what you really are inside; appearance ultimately plays the *subordinate* role. If you make your exterior the principal *you*, you are destined to overstate or understate it, continually confused about the "real you."

2. Once you've found your comfortable form of "simple," chose *one* area that becomes a trademark; spend a little fun time on it. This may involve finding the right perfume to fit your mood each day, or fussing with your hair for 15 minutes longer than necessary each morning, or changing your nail enamel to match your shoes. But "simple, plus" means you choose with care, not letting the game totally control your psyche.

3. Women who have too much to do and too little time should also choose the fabric of their clothes carefully. I sense there are still a lot of irons waiting on kitchen counters for their daily jobs. Irons have been almost unnecessary for the past ten years, so you don't *have* to depend on them. Of course, you *may* want to have a few beyond-simple items that do require pressing, but these clothes should be saved for times when you have the extra moments to spend rather than forming part of a Tuesday-morning warm-up act.

4. Be strong enough not to follow every fad and fancy in clothing that hits the women's page of the newspaper. Like most of us, you probably don't look good in everything, so be objective, ask your *true* friends for their opinions. Use some sense before you find yourself wearing a miniskirt into the boardroom!

5. Also, guard against Pat's mistake: Don't try to dress like a man. As we move into a traditionally male world, this is an easy error to make, but wearing men's clothing seldom has the desired effect.

One more point regarding "dress" remains to be made: cigarettes. Apart from smoking cigarettes, you wear them; they're part of your appearance.

Statistics show that as the numbers of women have increased on the job front, more and more of them are starting to smoke. The rising health hazard to women is, of course, of concern, but the health aspect is not the point here. The points are these:

1. Cigarettes irritate many people today, and smoking may annoy a number of people you'd rather not annoy. In addition to smoking's being generally offensive to many, there are a smaller number who still have a double standard about women smoking. Most wouldn't admit it, but it's there, nevertheless.

2. Many people (who perhaps consider themselves "pop psychologists") identify cigarette smoking as a sign of insecurity. It's something to do with your hands when you don't know what else to do. With all these reasons for smoking having been overdone in the press, many people now regard these hypotheses as facts.

3. Your smoke will frequently harm others physically. The smoke itself is very irritating to the eyes, nose, throat, taste, and smell of many non-smokers around you. You'll never realize how much others are tolerating because of you until you quit smoking.

4. If you must smoke, don't be the first one to light up in a new group. This is just a commonsense suggestion for those interested in making a good impression.

You, of course, are the one in charge of what you choose to wear. You may believe that "simple" lacks imagination altogether and that the way you look when you smoke is no one's business. Just remember: Your appearance is always talking, whether you want it to or not. Does it project the message you really want to send?

THE SOCIAL CLUB AT THE SHOP

In Chapter 2, we reviewed women's involvement in social organizations around the turn of the century. These women were very helpful to many causes, but the organizations themselves also gave women somewhere to go to get out of their own homes. These groups provided the company of other women for chatting and socializing. Many women who didn't belong to official organizations also spent hours getting together over coffee and their latest sewing projects. Given this history, it is not surprising that socializing has been considered part of the female domain.

As women began moving into the workforce, some of these needs and habits followed them. In her 1980 best-seller, *Unfinished Business*, Maggie Scarf concluded (to the dismay of many feminists) that women are "more people-oriented from the moment of birth"* anyway. If this is true, this natural inclination has had a lot of help from tradition and proximity in the workplace. Most of us spend a large percentage of our time on the job. The people we work with have an important influence on our lives.

Gossip

Historically, there was another reason for women to accentuate the social aspects of their jobs: There wasn't all that much job to do, particularly in the low-level ranks. Many days, there is still very little to do in low-paid jobs, yet the time must be spent. Of course, it is no secret that women still fill most of these jobs. Even when there is a lot of actual work to do, many women work without much satisfaction, responsibility, or enjoyment. It is therefore natural for them to take advantage of any chance they have to get away from tedium. Socializing provides the opportunity.

Men like to get into the act, too, and always have. But many men have traditionally held higher-level positions, with more demands and greater rewards. Time and inclination to participate in the office social scene have been less available, although they've learned to "work the network" for the advancements they need. There is, of course, a great difference between the contacts that lead to promotions and the general office social club. It's more important than ever for women to identify this difference if they hope to move into influential positions.

The image of women as frivolous social creatures must stop at some point if their comments are ever to be considered discussing instead of gossiping. There are numerous ways in which many women handle themselves in the social climate of the office that continue to work against them in their bid to be taken more seriously. One of our most destructive acts is gossip. Gossip is harmful to those we talk about and to us as well, for it diminishes us by broadcasting that we have nothing better to do.

Gossip is a dirty word that describes what other people do. Few of us would openly admit that we like to gossip. We've been told from day one that gossip isn't nice, but since we seemed to hear this from others who enjoyed gossiping, we tended to ignore the noble counsel.

Not only is gossip a time-waster; it is a people-destroyer as well. Even when people have all the facts, they can't repeat the information accurately. And of course, no one ever has all the facts. There can be 50 different factors that affect any given situation, which we can't possibly understand. It's totally unfair to harm someone else through gossip. Un-

* (Garden City, N.Y.: Doubleday, 1980), p. 535.

fortunately, the danger is seldom clear to us until we are the victim instead of the abuser.

Some of the most naive find it fun to talk about their boss. This is a double sin. Not only have they offended another human being, but they have violated a trust they accepted when they took the job that gave them access to privileged information. Talking negatively about your boss is a true Benedict Arnold act. It says more about you than it does about your boss, and the impression it gives about you is all negative. It makes you no better than the woman who constantly complains about her "old man" to her bored friends and neighbors.

I'm personally happy to find that more people I meet now hold their tongues. Perhaps this is because I tend to interact with people who have a lot to do—and who do it! It's probably not that they're above gossiping; it's simply that they have other things filling their minds—and have no time to clutter them with gossip and other unproductive trivia. Note this: The best cure for the tendency to gossip is to keep yourself involved in achieving important goals.

That Irritating Personality

Even if you learn not to talk about other people, there is usually at least one person you must work with whose personality and habits clash with yours. You can feel there's going to be trouble the first time you meet; later, you prove to yourself you were right. Everything that person does will irritate you; he (or she) will make your blood boil! You'll blame that person for mistakes you've made, delays you must tolerate, your head-aches, and your general unhappiness as well. You'll spend hours of your free time at home "telling her off." Some days are worse than others, but you frequently dream "How nice my life would be if only Harold weren't in it!"

In addition to the perception that women are gossipers, women are perceived as the sort who will let a particular personality get in their way. They allow this other person to emotionally upset them to such an extent that their work and their attitude both suffer. We should all strive to rise above this malady, although most of us have fallen victim to it at one time or another. Experience, fortunately, usually teaches us better ways to deal both with undesirable people and with undesirable feelings we find in ourselves.

Younger women report the most trouble with personality conflicts. One 22-year-old woman complained, "I don't like being treated like a fool by him!" At 24, another objected, "Older men think I'm so cute." One 22-

year-old customer service rep, who lives in Michigan, explained her problem this way:

> My frustrations begin with my inability to work closely with the one per-
> son I really should work closest with. Habits of his annoy me; our person-
> alities are drastically different; our senses of responsibility/reliability are
> also different. Try as I might, I find it difficult to work with someone I
> really don't like. Therefore, as I become frustrated, my work suffers. I
> become irritated, and sometimes reflect this back onto some undeserving
> soul.

The younger we are, the more likely we are to have limited views of
acceptable behavior. When we're young, we've had few opportunities to
be the odd woman out ourselves and are consequently very unsympathetic
to the seemingly strange activities of others. Then, too, we exalt our own
virtues (in the quote above, there's no question whose "sense of responsibility" the speaker perceives as greater!), and we tend to downplay the
skills and abilities of others. This tendency may stem from general insecurity and a need to prove ourselves. Also, when we're young, we're more
confident that we have the right answers and those who disagree with us
are simply wrong!

Sometimes older women complain about this tendency in younger
women, perhaps displaying the same intolerance they themselves find unacceptable. One woman (age 35) explained to me:

> Maybe it's the current trend, but it seems that the younger workers these
> days are just plain lazy. Women who want a good paycheck but are not
> willing to accept responsibility make it harder on the rest of us who must
> constantly help them along. The young girls in the office don't seem to
> want to learn how to improve anything they do. There is a good deal of
> bellyaching about their jobs. Also, they don't try to get along with other
> workers who have different personalities. There's a lot of unnecessary nit-
> picking just because of two or three differences of opinion. I try not to get
> too involved in any one person's quarrel with another. I'm getting paid to
> work, not negotiate truces. I try to be friends with everyone. That's hard
> because I don't get to see all the girls, but I try to keep up with them and
> their lives. I think, as the girls mature, they will learn to value their
> relationships with their fellow co-workers, and this situation will improve.

It seems it does improve with age. At age 48, this next woman's feelings are more representative of the comments concerning office interactions: "There are a lot of interruptions and some chauvinism, but
basically, my working conditions and the people are very good!"

What psychologists tell us is true: we cannot control what others do to us, but we can begin to control the way we react to what they do. This is a secret key to successful work-related encounters.

After running into many personality conflicts myself when I was young, I finally began playing a useful mental game whenever I started work in a new office community. I asked myself a day or two before I began, "Who's going to be the thorn in my side this time?" And of course, there was always someone to fill the role. The knowledge, however, that there would probably be one there took some of the sting out of actually meeting him or her. Once I began to successfully handle that type of person, the antagonist had less and less control over me; in fact, I began to enjoy it when such types moved through their routine!

There is *always* something you can learn or gain from your interactions with other people. Identify something you can learn from all people, so that interactions with them become beneficial instead of detrimental. Listen to another mature woman's comment on office interactions. She's had over 50 years of interacting with unpleasant personalities: "Understanding people helps soften most blows, since there is not much you can do to change them. Patience is *the* virtue!"

Most people aren't going to think the way you do. The traditional housewife had the same problem, although she had more time to bristle at the offenses of her sister, her mother-in-law, or her neighbor's dog. We end up taking ourselves too seriously, and we are the ones who suffer for it. Perhaps, in the end, we should take the advice of one fortyish woman who combined the two sides of herself by working out of her own home: "Happiness is being too busy to know how miserable you are!" Maybe it's also being too busy to let personality quirks become an issue.

Aggression: Subtle and Overt

Women have been taught to swallow their anger because it's "unladylike" to blow up or get mad. Most of us have learned this lesson well, successfully keeping our mouths shut while the anger grew inside. We have suffered because of this approach to our anger, turning much of our antagonisms inward. It frequently surfaced as anxieties, nerves, pimples, fat, cigarettes, nail-biting, exaggerated hand movement, and constant chattering. In its more severe outbreaks such repressed rage has led to ulcers and occasionally suicide.

Hidden anger in women also manifests itself in the form of unexpected attacks on our family and co-workers. Many of these attacks seem to be without provocation. Of course, this leads to miscommunication, for the people we attack have no idea what's wrong with us. Husbands complain about women who blow up for no apparent cause. One recently divorced man told me at a conference:

> I had no idea at all there was anything wrong with my marriage until I came home one night and she was packing. Then she let it all hang out— 100 things I'd done wrong over the past five years! I'd forgotten nearly all of it!

Children have the same problems. Their mothers take many of their frustrations out on their children because they can get away with it, or so it seems. Children are smaller and vulnerable, and frequently a little intimidated by their mothers (at least until they're teenagers). They get mixed signals, because the same actions on their part bring different responses from their moms. Leaving the orange juice glass on the piano is O.K. one day; it causes a tirade the next.

Subtle aggression is manifested in other ways. We carry grudges for a very long time. We may criticize boys and men who fight things out, but fighting frequently settles their problems. Our grudges, on the other hand lead to a complex plan of attack and counterattack; it can go on for weeks, months—even years. It takes endless energy, time, and attention. It's a very heavy load to carry, and we get tired of it.

Some women, as they have entered the world that once belonged to men, have decided to grab hold of one of the male world's most aggressive, least physical tools: swearing. It seems a good technique to many. You don't have to get physically violent; yet you can rip, tear, snarl, and snort. Many women who have adopted this approach to releasing their tensions will defend it stoutly as their right and privilege. "It's therapeutic!" some will claim. "Besides, I feel so damn much better when I let it all hang out."

Well, good for them. I believe it's childish and unattractive for either men or women. Swearing indicates a total lack of control, not a positive release of pent-up feelings. Swearing is bound to cause a new set of negative feelings and frustrations of its own, because negative conversation leads to further negative thinking and conversation. None of us improve our lot in life by adopting the less attractive ways of others. We frequently just look foolish.

And of course, I don't advocate that women fight it out in the ring or in the alley. Learning to throw punches isn't any smarter than throwing dirty words.

But everyone's bound to get really angry sometimes. How, then, do you handle aggressive feelings instead of internalizing them as we have usually done?

1. Learn to accept your anger. No one is happy all the time. Who'd want it anyway? Angry is one side of our range of emotions. Today is not a good day, and you're angry. So deal with it.

2. In most cases, it's not a good idea to explode on the spot. Sure, it sometimes feels good to scream immediately, but you're usually screaming and ranting at another person who is also upset and not thinking clearly. This situation is explosive and usually leads to statements better left unsaid. Unfortunately, once words are spoken, they cannot be unsaid, and the more negative comments linger in another person's memory forever, even though the conflict has been settled.

3. Although you shouldn't explode right away, neither should you forget to resolve the problem. It must be settled—*in the near future*. If you try to ignore it in order to avoid a confrontation, it will remain inside and eat away at you. The same situation will occur again, and bingo—you have the building blocks of a grudge and subtle aggravation.

It takes a certain amount of nerve and experience to bring your complaints up later. It's especially difficult because the best time to talk about such things is when everyone's in a good mood—and who wants to spoil good feelings with negative or disturbing thoughts? It must be done anyway, or the good times will get fewer and fewer as your frustrations continue to grow. Also, if you fail to settle the issue, paranoia may set in. You lose your sense of perspective when your hurts gnaw inward from failing to get them out in the open.

4. Get a pad and pen as soon as anger sets in. Write those frustrations down as fast as you can (go ahead, throw a dirty word in now and then, if you must!). Write everything you're thinking until you can write no more. Then stick it in your underwear drawer so no one else will see it. You'll feel better for expressing your anger, even if it is only on paper.

Vigorous exercise can also help. You've gotten your mental and emotional anger out; now work your physical anger out. A fast, determined walk does the trick for me. Others might prefer calisthenics, running, or a punching bag. Work up a sweat and talk to yourself.

In most cases, you should guard against getting rid of your anger by talking to another person. Many of us have lived to regret sobbing on someone else's shoulder; but then, many of us have at times been helped by the same technique. Just take care whom you talk to—and about what!

5. Let yourself "cool" for a day or so. Put your complaint on the back burner, but again—not for too long. Try to figure out what happened and why. Put yourself in the other person's position. What angers and frustrations were driving him or her? How did the frustrations grow?

6. Once you've given your gripe a chance to set, approach the "defendant." The right time is crucial and is frequently difficult to find. Then,

too, there's no guarantee that this is going to be easy, particularly if you've never taken this approach before and the other person is also hurt and angry.

The confrontation has the greatest chance of a happy conclusion if you can honestly see the other's point of view and share that fact with your foe. Let that person know that you're concerned about correcting the misunderstanding, not making trouble. Your goal is resolution, not a fight about something that happened days ago.

7. If you have had an explosion on day one, with both parties harboring hard feelings, and that famous "thick air" has set in, talking about it later is still a good technique. If the wound is not actively healed with words of understanding, the situation will get progressively worse.

8. You're never going to have an anger-free life, but you can minimize and dissipate the anger that does come your way. The key is to deal with it—before it consumes you and everything you want out of your home, your job, and your life.

"It Sounds Like a Woman!"

In general, women speak differently than men. While this difference is beneficial in some situations, it has been a problem for women in the business world. Most of us don't even think of our speaking and our voice as being either good or bad; they're just there. Our voice, and the way we use it, can nevertheless be crucial to our success or failure in our professional lives.

First impressions are always important, and nothing other than our general appearance has a greater impact on another person than our voice. Our voice transmits our first move toward another. Even more than touch, which most people don't get into for a long time, our voice reveals a lot about us and what we think of ourselves and others.

What does your voice say about you? Do you have any of the following problems that are common to women?

First of all, a woman's voice is frequently too _____, compared with a man's voice. You know many of the words that fill this blank: *shrill, soft, syrupy, sexy, gruff, irritating.* We seldom hear anyone say that a woman has a nice voice, although this comment is frequently made in reference to a male voice.

Unfortunately, these "too" tones get offensive and disturbing over a period of time. Nobody wants to listen to them, and thus, the method of communication ends up killing your chances of being heard.

You can change the quality of your voice if you really want to. It will take work, because most of us have been actively talking for a long time, but it can be done.

Analyze your voice. Do you talk too much, getting louder as you get more nervous or involved? Use a tape recorder, trying to talk normally; record your phone conversations or general office conversations. Listen to yourself critically.

Note carefully what you hear. If your voice is too high (many are), work to lower it. This can be done with a conscious effort, and you will like the results instantly yourself. Through determination, you can make this new voice your regular tone. "Lower" is more mellow and easier on everyone.

Also, note whether you use a lot of nervous bridges in your speech. Do you say "and a" a lot? Or "un-hun," "gee," or "O.K."?

Do you talk too slow or too fast? Both are offensive. If you talk too fast, people can't understand what you are saying. Some people slur words so much only their mothers could possibly understand them. On the other hand, women who speak too slowly put people to sleep. The audience loses interest before you get to your point.

Do you apologize when speaking? Do you say, "you know?" "if you want to," "I think," or "sort of" all the time? Do you make most things sound like a question instead of a definite statement?

Do you talk so quietly that no one can hear you? If you do, the impression will be that you don't want anyone to hear you; you'll sound afraid.

One of the most professionally detrimental habits associated with women is giggling. It signals a lack of confidence. A confident person will say, "It's hot in here!" and proceed to open a window. A less-than-confident person will say, "Gee, does it seem a little warm in here to you? Or is it just me? (Tee-hee, tee-hee!) Would any of you mind if I open this window just a crack? Would you mind, George? Would you mind, Sally? I'll close it if the snow blows in. (Tee-hee, tee-hee!)" Get the picture?

If women talk in this manner, how can they expect someone to listen to them? Studies consistently show that men interrupt women far more than women interrupt men, but if women continue to apologize, back off, and giggle, why shouldn't men interrupt? Most of us will readily interrupt babies if we think we have something more important to say. Hard as it may be to accept, men take the same advantage of insecure speech in women.

The secret is self-confidence. Self-confidence is difficult to attain, but in regard to speech, you can sound more self-confident by watching and imitating the speech of confident women. Look for these women and listen to them wherever you can. You'll learn more from them than if you simply try to imitate a particularly powerful man, although watching the way men speak can also be beneficial.

Learn to project yourself. Speak directly to the person you're talking to and listen carefully to what the person says so you can respond. Stop being so self-conscious. Learn to speak directly and respond directly to the situation at hand. Once you truly show yourself you can do it, you'll feel the power generated by your performance.

Women and Criticism

Competitive situations, such as those you get into when you enter the business world, require a thick skin. Unfortunately, women have a reputation for having a thin skin. Criticism is a major part of the workaday world, and women traditionally take it badly. We're all familiar with the typical response: the quivering lip at the first negative comment, the furrowed brow as the explanation of the problem continues, the inevitable sniffling, and finally, the downpour of tears. All of this may be hard to control, but it gets in your way when you fail to control it. Many men hesitate to criticize or talk honestly to women because of the reputation women have for getting upset easily. Few people can handle tears. Tears absolutely cut off communication and are very frustrating. They cause embarrassment for everyone involved, followed by a papering over of the problem "so the little lady will feel better." When this happens, the crying victim may feel somewhat relieved if she has avoided further critical remarks, but her relief is unfounded. She is in more trouble than ever, because she has shown there's little chance of improvement. She can't talk about her mistakes.

Learning to take criticism well is an essential skill. Since anyone who tries anything is going to make mistakes, it's important to learn about these mistakes and grow from the experience. If you're going to learn from your mistakes, criticism from others is essential; you can't figure it all out yourself.

Of course, you don't like to make mistakes. No one does. We all make them anyway. It really is possible to accept your mistakes without turning on the faucet. But how?

First of all, accept your limitations. You weren't made a faultless human being. And when you err, you had better believe others are going to notice. They're busy looking for your mistakes so they won't feel so isolated by their own. If a person finds something to criticize, listen to him or her. That person will probably say something important that will help you learn about yourself. Of course, some people can present criticism in a nice way, while others cannot, but you don't have a choice as to who criticizes you. Listen attentively even to the most severe critic: He or she may have the biggest lesson of your life ringing in the air; don't lose it because your hearing is muffled by sobs.

You can stop those tears welling up in your eyes if you want to. Fill your mind. Think of ways of changing, for the better. If this doesn't do it, figure out why the person felt a need to approach you. If neither of these thoughts successfully lowers the tide in your brimming eyes, it's time to stop trying to learn from the experience and simply concentrate on *keeping those tears from coming*. At least save yourself from making a bad situation worse by turning it into a full-scale tearjerker. Think of anything ridiculous or funny. If you cry a lot and easily, develop a tear-stopping joke. When the scene gets heavy, concentrate on it. You may not learn anything from the situation, and you may still have to face the music, but at least you won't cry. Not crying takes a lot of practice, but a thicker skin is well worth the effort. You'll be more comfortable, and so will everyone else.

Once a negative experience is over, don't brood about past mistakes. It seems that most women I know are plagued (instead of blessed) with a good, detailed memory. They focus hard, and they remember. They particularly remember their mistakes. They almost love to dwell on them, replaying them over and over again in their minds. Of course, this is foolish. This leads to a detrimental activity second only to giggling—whining. It's "poor me," put to song. It's irritating to anyone who has to hear it and gets tiresome as soon as it begins. It's also hard to know when you're doing it. The best approach is to stop complaining about what's wrong or difficult. Look for your strengths and learn to develop them. Become a positive person. When you do, the negatives will slip off easily as you accept them, learn from them, and release them. Knock the chip off your shoulder. Of course you have special problems, but so does the next person. Quit brooding and get on with it.

Sex in the Office

No other single issue causes as much gossip and as many potential problems as sex in the office. This issue speaks to the heart of women's problems as they try to move beyond the traditional female stereotypes to something more. Some say sex in the office is the national pastime. The job has replaced the coffee shops and the bars, the church socials and the roller rinks as the most fertile mating ground.

Most office romances end badly, especially for the woman, who usually has less to start with in the first place. Unfortunately, women also have farther to fall when things go sour. Women aren't new at this game, but the idea that women can win something at it *is* new. This idea is a little foolish, for there is still a double standard. In every sense of the word, sex in the office is a powerful issue that frequently harms the parties involved, particularly the women.

There are five basic types of male/female relationships on the job front. They deserve a little exploring.

Type A: Easy Friendship. We'll start here as opposed to spending a lot of time exploring the hostile, negative interactions between some men and women, although some of the more intimate relationships actually reflect these destructive sentiments rather than endearing feelings.

A Type A relationship is pleasant and easy. There's a sense of admiration between the two parties, tempered with respect. Both the man and the woman are aware that the other is of the opposite sex; it just doesn't make that much difference. Easy friendship leaves no maddening residue. Both parties can feel comfortable around each other. They are friends and glad to know each other.

From here on, it's downhill all the way.

Type B: Flirtations and Sexual Jokes. It's just one step from Type A to Type B, but it's a big step. It's a major move, for it sets you on an entirely different level of interaction.

Type Bs enjoy playing peek-a-boo with each other. Their flirtations add a little spark to the day. Sexual jokes and innuendos provide the spice. Everyone laughs outwardly, hiding some confusions inside. It's more fun for some than for others. In many cases, it's the first step to sexual put-down. It begins defining woman's "place."

Type C: Making Passes. The hankie-pankie begins. Words have moved to physical advances at the water cooler and in the elevators. Type C behavior is the last stop before the bus heads out of town.

Type D: Pastime Affairs. These are those little *tête-à-têtes* that supposedly harm no one. Type D behavior is what many sophisticates suggest is a reasonable indoor sport, as long as you don't let it get too serious. Pastime affairs require that you use your body as a recreational vehicle. These affairs are good for a few laughs until someone blows it all by feeling guilty or getting involved.

Type E: Involvement—Deeply in It. Type Es frequently begin as Type Ds, but something happens. The situation gets out of hand for one or both parties. What was supposed to be something simple becomes something more. The couple is truly *in* an involvement.

What's happened here? Do people really intend to hurt and use each other? Do they really care that little about what they're doing to themselves and to others?

Of course, there's a big difference between affairs of single people and affairs of married people. Singles are playing for themselves, so they can lose and win for themselves. Their moral values are their own business, and they're putting no one else on the line but themselves. They aren't breaking a critical commitment to another person or persons by their actions, although they may be breaking a number of generally accepted standards of the business community, thus harming all businesspersons through their unprofessional conduct. Ginger Tate, a prosperous sales rep from Denver, shares her experience and insight into office affairs:

> When I began selling, I was divorced and must admit I did not handle men on the job well. I met a few that were quite sexually attractive, and we did have affairs. It is a very awkward situation after the affair has ended. While neither were customers, I still have interactions with these men—one is still seeking to continue the relationship (sexually) and I have to continually fight it. The other man and I seem to handle our friendship fine. But I feel it was a poor move on my part to succumb to the sexual temptation. But it's tough if you're single and you meet stimulating men.
>
> About two years into my selling career, I knew I wasn't going to allow myself to become sexually involved with business associates and then controlled the situations accordingly. Some men respect that. Others naturally regret it. I must say I regretted it, too. I consider my sexual standards to be quite free. And it's unfortunate the business community sets its own standards. I guess that's one of the rules you learn to play by.
>
> Now that I'm married, I have no desire for a sexual relationship with another man. Men ease up on married women, but they still think they have a chance with you, and they continue to try in their own subtle ways. Fortunately, no one has threatened to take away business from me if I didn't sleep with them, and I know I wouldn't do it, but it would certainly deflate my faith in the business community if that occurred.

As Ginger suggested, married women are not beyond sexual temptations on the job, and married people who become sexually involved put themselves in double jeopardy. Marrieds are even more severely sanctioned for their extramarital involvements, because they are betraying both personal and professional standards. They display the childish tendency of putting themselves ahead of all other concerns.

Why do these affairs happen so frequently?

I believe that Type B, Type C, and Type D interactions frequently develop from a state of confusion, for a little diversion, and for a few laughs. Men and women are uncomfortable both with themselves and with the members of the opposite sex with whom they must rub shoulders daily. They easily revert to the type of interactions they believe they're supposed to use with the opposite sex. The "what feels good is good" attitude that has developed in the past 40 years topples many of the old barriers. Productivity may fall, but some of the workers are having fun, usually at the expense of other workers and family members.

I don't believe most people are intentionally destructive; they just get caught up in a situation they fail to understand. They confuse job, proximity, and commitment.

We spend a great deal of time on our jobs, and if we're lucky, we get involved in what we're doing. The work becomes important to us, and thus, when the same work is important to another, we develop a bond. Concern for the project is transferred from the work to other persons: This common concern combines with our traditional ways of interacting between males and females, and the situation gets sticky. Of course, it all isn't as trite as "love my project, love me," but the issue of empathy and understanding plays a very important role.

This scenario happens easily to a married woman when she first begins to work again after a period of being isolated at home. These women have been in a protected environment: at home for years, in elementary schools where there are few men, or in other, mostly women situations. The first-timers are not used to being known for doing something themselves, apart from their husbands. Suddenly, with a new job, they find they have the opportunity to know another man without being attached. This isn't to say they hide the fact that they are married; it's just a new experience to meet other men without the security (and barrier) of a husband in view. This initial encounter can be very confusing. Sometimes the experience goes no farther than the woman's imagination, but it can be bothersome, nevertheless. For the first time, she may feel slightly wicked. She can't understand the feelings that are moving inside her, and she's afraid. She's often incapable of keeping these feelings a secret, particularly if she's used to being an open person. She gets flustered when "the other man" enters the room. She makes mistakes she usually doesn't make. She finds it difficult to talk. Her mind is filled with this new person, both at work and at home.

An observant husband will notice. This can compound the problem if he reacts negatively, for then the woman has the reality of her husband's predictably annoyed reaction, compared with the dream of her new "lover."

The plot thickens when the object of her affection returns her interest. The problem becomes real when they finally slip away together, and another "undying love" is born.

Of course, we can write different endings for different love stories, but the sad part of this well-worn tale is that most renditions end unhappily.

If a woman's involvement in a romance has aided her advancement on the job (known as "sleeping your way to the top"), there are other pipers to pay. Everyone will know about the affair and disapprove, particularly if the promoted party is getting more from this affair than someone else is getting from hers. If her advancement requires additional management responsibilities, the new manager will have still more problems, because not only will she lack the respect of her subordinates but they will frequently try to make her look bad in her new role.

The woman who wins with female wiles has also put herself in a precarious dependency situation. She definitely owes her mentor and will have trouble paying her debt. She frequently gets into more trouble than she can handle when her lover starts to feel guilty because he's married (and he usually is) or he gets tired of her (and he usually does). Then he gets angry. It's the classic no-win situation. Unfortunately, this woman has also added to the problems of us all. The reputation and integrity of women in general suffers from the selfish acts of women such as these.

What's good for a flutter or two of the heart is disaster when tested with additional intimacy, especially after the newness has worn off. The fling may be fun, but the finales aren't fun at all. Most of the heart palpitations will go away when you look at the situation objectively. Contrary to the dreams of many 15-year-old girls, there's not a one and only. There are many people we can find attractive, and it is highly likely we will be attracted to many men in our lifetime, particularly if we meet many men. It only takes certain circumstances to make this attraction become something more. Your decision rests on how you deal with these complicated feelings.

You can learn to handle these situations successfully if you want to. Stop watching so much television and reading so many romances. Realize that your attraction is not The Great Love of the Century. It's timing, circumstances, and a little heavy breathing. That's it. Ask yourself what price you'd have to pay to follow this sidetrack. Consider the price as objectively as you can, because it will likely be the most costly decision of your life.

You aren't an evil person for having warm feelings for another person; these feelings are common and very natural. We all hope our lives will be filled with people who make us feel particularly joyful and happy. It's very special to admire others for what they are and what they've accomplished.

But it should stop there. Whenever possible, try to involve a third or fourth party in your activities. If you're married, take your mate to the office party or don't go. Leave any situation when the drinking begins to show in the behavior of the group. Draw the "no nonsense" line and stick to it!

Whatever you do, don't play games. You don't have to be stern and serious; you can have a good time and be lighthearted. Just leave flirting to teenagers. You look silly sending mixed signals, planning to play a little—but not a lot.

It might help us all to look at these compromising situations a little more objectively when we realize just how much women have suffered because someone sent flowers or said the three magic words. The strongest resolve can be shattered when a man says, "You are really something!" "Do you *know* what you do to me?" "I can't live without you," or—the ultimate killer—"I love you." Women have jumped off cliffs after hearing the sound of those words. What power this gives a man who knows how to use such words well, particularly when accompanied by the appropriate looks and actions of love!

Do I sound cynical? I think I do. Unfortunately, I've seen it happen, and so have most of you. I love being in love, and I love knowing someone loves me. I wish everyone could experience a true love in their lifetime. But I also hate seeing women get taken by men who misuse love and the power the dream of love has over so many women. I hate, most of all, to see women trap themselves because of their fantasies, which are fed regularly by the media. I die a little when I see either men or women throwing everything of true value in their lives down the drain because of some vision of eternal romantic bliss. And I get truly angry when I think of all the other people who have paid for their dreams! The spouse who must adjust to the mate's wanderings, the children who are forced to manage far more than they're prepared to handle, and all the friends and relatives who are left to pick up the pieces. And I'm sorry for the lovers themselves, because with few exceptions, they'll wake up one morning and realize they have nothing more than they had before. If children were involved, they've paid a price they can't recover.

Karen Adams, a 43-year-old sales rep with three teenage sons, sounds confident when she says:

> I'm not tempted by men on the job. As a saleswoman, my manner is always so professional that no one ever made a pass at me. (And I'm very attractive.) There is a sexual "awareness" once in a *great* while, but *very* harmless stuff. Sex in the office is no problem at all for me. If you send out sexual signals, you get them back!

Later in our conversation, Karen told me how she's "strong in a man's world." Her statement held some of the secrets to her ability to achieve uncomplicated success in working with men:

> I never utter anything about problems. A bright, competent, professional manner is what does it. Brisk and confident is a winner. Men understand that.

I agree; men do understand that. They can tell when the answer will be a sound "no" even before asking. Once this is determined, both of you can get on with the business at hand.

The issue here is a conscious stand. It has nothing to do with falling in love. As responsible individuals, we know there will be temptations throughout our lives. They're a regular feature of living. Our personal success or failure comes from the choice we make at decision time. Here is the true measure of success in men or women. No one said it was going to be easy, but then, the fact that an issue involves a hard decision is not sufficient justification for making the easy choice. Skip the esoteric discussion about situational ethics. We all know the decision we should make when we find ourselves getting into a tangled office romance. In the long run, we, too, will be happiest with the decision that sees beyond the unrealistic dream of the present moment.

There is a lot of the stereotyped woman in each of us, but there is also something better. Many of the traditional behaviors we have suffered with and enjoyed for hundreds of years are still valid—to a point. Many of them will have to bend as we now move toward another aspect of ourselves—an aspect that makes us directly involved in the economy.

We will continue to have problems with our friends and family, balancing their demands against our work, and hopefully keeping them from having a negative influence on our work. Our image will take on a different appearance, as we begin to reflect externally the many changes that are happening inside us. Finally, the way we interact with other people will change, for many of the old behaviors kept us from realizing our full potential. With a little help from others and a lot of help from ourselves, we'll leave some of the excess baggage behind, moving forward with the absolute best we have to offer.

5

NEW BEHAVIORS THAT GET YOU WHERE YOU WANT TO GO

OR

Get me another cup of coffee, Harry!

Despite the problems many of us have with stereotyped behaviors, the number of women moving into managerial ranks is increasing. Our numbers have almost tripled since 1960 to more than 3 million. Between 1960 and 1982, the number of female managers grew 175 percent, while the number of male managers grew 37 percent. Of course, there are still more male managers, but the balance is shifting at a rapid rate.

Who are these women who are making it? What special skills or attributes do they have in common that have helped them achieve their successes?

I have talked to hundreds of women about this issue. Frequently, it's easy to see why they've been successful: They have an air of confidence; they're obviously intelligent; they're open and meet you head-on. I've directly asked many of these women: "What is the secret of your success? Do you have any rules or guidelines you can share with other women?"

Many of them, ignoring tendencies to paranoia (self-confidence, again), were more than happy to share their thoughts with me. Their thoughts, combined with my own observations over the years, can be comfortably discussed under five headings:

Healthy Disrespect
Competition Exists—Face It!

Learning to Delegate Effectively
Meet Deadlines
The Female Managerial Role—You're It!

HEALTHY DISRESPECT

My concept of healthy disrespect has been developing since I was 15 years old. Back in the early 1960s, I'd walk past the teachers' lounge in my high school, wondering what advanced level of intellectual conversation went on behind that closed door—the door no students were permitted to enter. Then one day in my senior year, the school principal asked me to take a message to one of the teachers—in the teacher's lounge! I knocked gingerly on the door, and finally one of the coaches boomed: "Quit knocking and come in!" Cautiously I opened the door, and as the coach motioned for me to enter the sacred room, I did so, with fear and trembling. I waited—and observed—while Mrs. Miller read the principal's note and wrote her reply.

What an eye-opener this insignificant task turned out to be for me! No high-level intellectual conversation here! The teachers were drinking coffee and cokes, puffing on their cigarettes, gossiping and complaining—just like ordinary people! I had only imagined teachers were superior to other human beings!

I still had lessons to learn, however. When I got to college, I believed college deans must be beyond all reproach. How intelligent they must be to have achieved such a position! Of course, I learned many things from numerous professors and deans as well, but I continued to be somewhat intimidated by the level of their accomplishments. They were superior to me—or so I thought.

Then one day I heard that the dean at my school was being fired, but the administration had decided to let him "choose to retire" instead. "What's happening here?" I wondered, determined to find out. And I did find out. This man was a drunk and had been for many years. His last great accomplishment had been to graduate from a prestigious eastern school, over 40 years before. Since that time, he had gradually taken to the bottle, while all his work had been successfully handled by a few competent secretaries. This incident served as the climax to other, similar observations I had made over the years. The point was this: Many of the "big shots" whom I had judged to be so much better than I weren't really all that outstanding. I had forced myself to feel unworthy and unimportant when I negatively compared my paltry accomplishments with their great ones!

After observing many similar incidents in the business world, I finally coined a term that has helped me gain confidence wherever I go. The term is *healthy disrespect*. It's healthy because I acknowledge that I should maintain respect for all people, just because they're human beings. I should also remember to respect and acknowledge true accomplishments, for there are many good and talented people in this world who belong to all races and both sexes. But I should *not* let my evaluation of their success hem me in! I should realize that much of their success is due to the fact that they stuck with something for a very long time, worked hard, or maybe were just lucky. They, too, have their weaknesses and their problems. They are not totally secure in their decisions at all times; in fact, they all frequently make mistakes. And I used to think only I made mistakes!

Many women put all men on such a pedestal. They believe everything a man does will tend to be much better than anything a woman (particularly themselves) can hope to do. They look at the male's pin-striped suit and other trappings of authority and shudder, bowing to the superior strength, power, and intelligence of the man.

Some men, of course, are far more talented than everyone, other men as well as women. (Some women outshine everyone, too.) Many men, however, start out as insecure as anybody else, but if they have a chance to make decisions, they will make mistakes—and learn from them. Once they've learned by feeling (or bluffing) their way through various difficult situations, they get used to it—and move on to the next plateau with confidence. There's nothing inherent in men that makes them better. There is seldom anything inherent in any successful people that makes them winners—except that all-important ability to keep going, in spite of problems.

Certainly, there are some people who are smarter than you. So what? Those same smart people have shortcomings somewhere, even if they are not readily visible. We don't know everything about other people anyway; we know only what we think we see. It's pure foolishness to let these superficial and inaccurate impressions keep us down, and such ideas do keep us down so often. Everyone has insecurities about various things, and the effects of these insecurities fluctuate from day to day. Learn from other people; take what you can. But for heaven's sake, don't let their accomplishments weigh on you, intentionally or otherwise! Incorporate healthy disrespect into your thinking and get moving!

COMPETITION EXISTS—FACE IT!

Many people, men and women alike, bristle when they run into office politics. They feel disgusted, as though they're shocked to see it exists.

They act indignant and righteously state how grand life would be without it. They try to back off from politics, frequently feeling rather smug if they're not tainted by it all.

These people seldom get very far. No matter what we wish, office politics is here to stay. Some people are chosen, and others are not. Since there aren't enough upper berths for everyone, choices must be made regarding who gets them and who doesn't. We all say we want the ones with the real ability to get the advancements. This sometimes happens, but who is deserving is a very subjective judgment and is not easily determined. Somebody whom one person may think deserving and capable may not impress another person at all. There are many factors, and a person who wants to rise in the corporation must be willing to be involved in corporate gamesmanship. Period.

Being female complicates the entire issue. As women, we fight all the stereotypes described in the last chapter. Some are more of a problem than others. One of the most helpful abilities any woman can cultivate is the ability to figure out how the decision makers think. Frequently these decision makers are older men. We must realize that many have very old-fashioned ideas about women, yet they have been forced to acknowledge the accomplishments of many women. It's useful to find ways to impress these gentlemen, without getting into bed with them literally or figuratively. Brownnosing is too obvious, and screwing is dangerous and stupid. Besides, both these techniques are easily seen through and usually work to a woman's disadvantage. Fortunately, there are other, more honorable ways to go about the business of making an impression.

The first sincere way to make an impression is to look to others for help. Pick brains. Dig for secrets. There are reasons other people succeed, and you can develop these same skills once you know what they are. Those who ask for help and are willing to take advice usually get it.

The ability to learn from the experiences of others requires a certain amount of maturity. There is a tendency for many of us to perceive ourselves as unique—thus beyond learning from others. Yes, we're unique, but all of us have many similar qualities. Those who can start where another generation left off and move beyond finding out everything for themselves are the most successful.

Work constantly to improve your skills. Improve your level of education to give yourself the competitive edge. Would further training or a graduate degree help you? If you don't know for certain, ask those who do know.

We can all learn from mentors, but it's important to pick a mentor carefully. Ask yourself who was the mentor's teacher, what sort of reputation the proposed mentor has, and how well your personality and values fit in with the mentor's. Will he or she be a true help or a hindrance in the long run?

I personally believe female mentors are the most helpful to other females. There are problems, however, because there just aren't that many women available. Then, too, some women are unwilling to share their insights, particularly if they have worked their way to the top without help.

Male mentors can likewise be very helpful but also potentially dangerous. Of course there's always the danger of becoming too intimately involved, thus creating a professional liability for yourself instead of an asset. There's even the possibility that other people will *think* a physical relationship exists when none does. This, too, can be dangerous. We shouldn't be particularly concerned with what other people think, but people's thoughts are also part of office politics.

While you're learning from others, remember to rely on yourself. Develop your ability to get along with people. This task is simple, yet complicated. Some people naturally have more ingratiating personalities than others, but the ability to come across in a pleasant manner can be cultivated. One of the best ways to develop this skill is to convince yourself to be honestly and genuinely interested in other people. Phonies should stay home when it comes time for this one, because insincere interest is easily detected and frequently backfires. How do you learn to be sincere? Get to know a "useless" person—one you think has nothing to teach you. Find ways to interact with this person. Soon you *will* learn something, and it could be a very valuable lesson. When this happens once, you will find it increasingly easy to believe there is something to learn from everyone. Remember: You learn nothing when your mouth is open. When your ears are open, it's a different story.

Become committed and demonstrate a commitment to your work. Look at it as more than just a job. Your commitment will put you ahead of the competition. As long as you have to spend so many hours on something anyway, you might as well decide to like it. Find a joy in your work, and you will naturally discover ways to improve it. Once you start improving what you do, others (important others) will notice.

Following this point, don't be afraid to be innovative in your work. Those who produce at the minimally acceptable level seldom advance rapidly. Sure, they're dependable employees, but they don't *progress!* Take risks. Look for far-out ways to do what you do better. Don't be hemmed in by the way things have always been done. If you can make more of your job than has ever been made of that position before, you're bound to outshine the competition and be rewarded for your efforts.

Unfortunately, many women shy away from competition. They're uncomfortable with it and will gravitate to less threatening situations. Many would rather have each person judged on his or her own merit—competing, yes, but competing with themselves instead of with others.

If you don't compete, you don't win. Competition is very much a part of what the working world is all about and is one of the major stumbling blocks when we talk about women getting ahead.

Competition is made doubly hard because it is not part of the stereotyped female behavior. This means those women who learn to compete satisfactorily are frequently called unladylike or masculine. We all know an aggressive female is termed bitchy and uptight. So, along with competitive feelings, we must develop a hard shell that protects and insulates us from the direct and indirect name-calling. The trick is to grow that hard shell without becoming cynical and too tough for our own good.

Women who hope to compete successfully must learn to put their best foot forward without apologizing for it. They must learn to tell others—specifically those others who count—exactly what they can do well. This is not bragging; it's simply being confident enough about yourself to let it show.

It's also important to know how to make others feel good when they're around you. This is even more likely to allow others to feel positive and impressed—by you. The ability to make others feel good is very useful, since so few people know how to do it properly. It does not involve a lot of phony compliments; rather, it grows from a sincere respect and interest.

Learn to seize the initiative. Make the first move. This action also goes against the grain of many of us. You can help yourself get the courage, however, if you remember how you were asked to the prom. You watched the phone and passively waited for Prince Charming to call. How degrading!

Organize your own prom and ask your own date. If you have a reason to get together with someone, male or female, ask the person to attend with you, whether the event is a discussion over lunch or a business meeting in the next town. You don't have to hesitate, always waiting to be chosen. Do the choosing yourself.

Competing with women is uncomfortable both for many men and for other women as well. Competing and negotiating with men is the more common and familiar experience. Many men hate to compete and negotiate with women for just this reason. They're unsure of themselves. Many have false expectations of women, somehow believing they're all alike. Many men hate to confront women because they realize they have a tendency to defer to women, having been taught their manners at mother's knee. Don't be overly concerned about this advantage, however. Many women were also taught at their mother's knee to believe men were smarter—and the leaders. These false impressions make everything a little more exciting, challenging, and unpredictable. Just don't be the one to drop the advantage.

Surely we have certain problems when it comes to the game of competition, but we also have many advantages. Accentuate the advantages and ignore the disadvantages. Learn your way around and find the person who is really in charge of making decisions. Lay all groundwork and sell your idea to that person.

Most of all, knock the chip off your shoulder. It's a heavy burden for anyone. It keeps us from performing at our best. Compete as a person, not as a woman. This means putting the best self forward, without complaints and excuses.

LEARNING TO DELEGATE EFFECTIVELY

Getting promotions and advancing in any company usually involves the responsibility of managing people. Managing people, of course, requires the art of delegation. Unfortunately, many women have trouble with delegation. They hesitate to tell other people what to do. Some are insecure. Some fear a bossy reputation. Some had work dumped on them by their own supervisors in the past and don't want to do the same thing to their subordinates.

Since delegation skills are crucial to your advancement in most jobs, however, women must learn to delegate effectively. Let's take a closer look at why women are frequently hampered in their efforts to delegate.

First of all, many have an undying desire for perfection. "It must be done right, and the only one you can count on is yourself!" is a frequent feeling. Ann Adams, a 33-year-old human resources manager from Denver, puts it this way: "I can do it quicker and better than anyone else, so why should I train others?"

In a way, Ann has a point. She probably *can* do it quicker and better than her subordinates, at least at first. What she fails to note in this attitude is that, as a manager, it is her job to do more *planning*, while training her subordinates to perform the tasks that carry out her plan. As a person goes up the managerial ladder, it is always her job to do more planning and less doing. The woman who fails to realize this is digging a grave for her career. You must let go of the subordinates' duties.

As a manager, it is also part of your responsibility to develop those below you, and this means teaching them new skills. Yes, you're still responsible, but you must learn to be responsible for what *they* do.

The second reason many women fail to delegate properly is that they frequently have an ambiguous understanding of what their job entails. Ann exemplifies this point by writing:

> After I got my promotion, I found I had a real problem. Good ole' Annie had always done *a, b,* and *c,* so everyone expected that I would continue to do these things—plus my new duties. After all, I'd done them for so long, everyone figured it wouldn't take me very long to continue to do them. I, myself, was also uncertain what I should continue to do.

Obviously, a clear-cut job description is in order. Many companie do not have them, however, so it is important for the newly appointed manager to actively seek a clear definition of her job. Many women have special problems if they have good secretarial skills. Noting these skills, upper management often assumes she can do her own clerical work, whereas a male manager wouldn't be expected to do so.

Some women have kept their secretarial skills a secret for just this reason. Others can't keep them a secret, particularly if they are working in a company where their skills are well-known. The only answer to this is an aggressive effort to get secretarial help. This is difficult, but if you generate enough productive activity, your need for secretarial help will become obvious—and you should get it, even if you have to holler. Once you get the assistance you need, however, you can occasionally use your secretarial skills to save yourself time. It is frequently easier, for example, to beat out a quick letter on the typewriter yourself than to go through the procedures of having your secretary type it for you. Be careful of this, however. It's a common trap. Before you start typing again, be certain you've trained your secretary to handle some very important functions that are also essential to the running of the office.

Another reason many women fail to delegate effectively is the fear of criticism. We don't want others to think we're trying to tell them what to do, nor do we want our superiors to criticize us for the poor performance of our subordinates. Ann states:

> I feel so *responsible* for the work getting done and will do it personally rather than let something fall short of plan. Of course, some people take advantage of me because of this.

People probably do take advantage of Ann, since they know she's afraid something will go wrong. Also, if she is performing many of the tasks herself, she is also subject to criticism because she should be delegating, not doing. The criticism will not always be as direct as it is for obvious mistakes; it's just less likely she'll continue to get promotions if she fails to measure up to the demands of delegation.

A big help here is learning to take criticism positively. O.K., so you're a little embarrassed at being questioned on something that was done improperly by a subordinate. Grow from the errors, don't hide from them. Next time, take care to see that this problem is corrected. Learn well from your mistakes.

The fourth reason women fail to delegate properly is that they lack confidence—both in others and in themselves. They are afraid their subordinates simply can't do a good job. On the other hand, they're sometimes afraid subordinates will do too good a job and outshine them. Ann shares her fears on this point:

> I'm afraid my organization will not value my ability as a manager when the results of my work are seen through the work of others, not through my individual contribution.

We all have insecurities, and these thoughts are understandable, but they're not justified. Good, productive activity in a department happens by plan, not by accident, and anyone who has made it to the top knows this is true. When your department is running smoothly, it's because someone is doing something right at the helm. If you're the one running the show, somebody on top will know it! You look good when your people look good.

How Well Do You Delegate?

How fine-tuned are your managerial skills? Can you delegate work effectively? Test yourself by answering yes or no to the following 15 questions:

1. Do you allow your people to make mistakes?
2. Do your people get promotions at least as frequently as others with equivalent responsibility in your organization?
3. Do you often take work home or work late at the office?
4. Does your operation function smoothly when you're absent?
5. Do you spend more time working on details than you do on planning and supervision?
6. Do your people feel they have sufficient authority over personnel, finances, facilities, and other resources?
7. Is your follow-up procedure adequate?
8. Do you overrule or reverse decisions made by your subordinates?

9. Do you bypass your subordinates by making decisions that are part of their jobs?
10. Do you do several things that your subordinates could—and should—be doing?
11. If you were incapacitated for six months, is there someone who could readily take your place?
12. Do your key people delegate well to their own subordinates?
13. Will there be many things requiring your action when you return from a trip or absence?
14. Do your subordinates take the initiative in expanding their authority with delegated projects without waiting for you to initiate all assignments?
15. When you delegate, do you specify the results you expect?

Give yourself one point for each "yes" answer to Nos. 1, 2, 4, 6, 7, 11, 12, 14, and 15. Give yourself one point for each "no" answer to Nos. 3, 5, 8, 9, 10, and 13. A good score is anything above 12. *

Guidelines for Better Delegation

No one can tell you exactly how to delegate. Each woman has her own job to consider, her own personality and ability, as well as the personalities and abilities of those below her. There are, however, certain guidelines that can help you become a better delegator. These guidelines suggest that you: (1) analyze your job; (2) decide what to delegate; (3) plan the delegation; (4) select the right person; (5) make the delegation; and (6) follow up on the delegated activity.

1. *Analyze Your Job.* Ask youself some important questions, such as, "What are my objectives?" "What results are expected of me?" "What do I do?" "Can anyone else do it for me?" "Can anyone be trained to do it?"

To help you analyze your job, prepare your delegation profile. On the top of a page, list the things you have already delegated. Second, list the things you could delegate. Third, list the things you're uncertain about delegating. Fourth, list the things you cannot delegate.

Once you have made these lists and thought about them carefully, discuss your analysis with your superiors. Obtain agreement or a working consensus with them. You can proceed more successfully once this is done.

2. *Decide What to Delegate.* How do you know what to delegate? Review your delegation profile. Consider delegating decisions you make most

* This quiz as well as many thoughts on delegation were taken from *The Time Management Workbook* (Time Management Center, 7612 Florissant Road, St. Louis, MO 63121, 1980), p. 56.

often, functions that make you overspecialized, areas in which your staff are better qualified, areas you dislike (taking care not to dump all unpleasant responsibilities on your subordinates), and activities that will add variety to your subordinates' jobs. Try to be fair and objective in your evaluation.

3. *Plan the Delegation.* Look at the whole job as a unit. What are you responsible for? Consider the various details and performance standards. What feedback is required? How often? How should this feedback come to you? What sort of training will be involved? And finally, if you can't control it, don't delegate it.

4. *Select the Right Person.* Find out the interests and intents of the people you supervise. What are their true abilities? What abilities can be developed? Who enjoys a challenge, and who does not? Is it possible to balance and rotate various teams?

Realize that there are several levels of delegation. Authority is delegated in differing degrees, although the differing degrees have frequently been neglected. When the degree of delegation has not been considered, a subordinate's responsibility may exceed the authority to act. The result? Unrealistic expectations, increasing interruptions, and a lot of wasted time for everyone.

Before you actually select a person to take over some of your tasks, consider these levels of delegation:

Level 6: Take action—no further contact with me required.
Level 5: Take action—let me know what you intend to do; do it unless I say no.
Level 4: Look into the problem—let me know what you intend to do; do it unless I say no.
Level 3: Look into the problem—let me know what you intend to do; don't take action unless I approve.
Level 2: Look into the problem—let me know possible alternative actions, include pros and cons of each, and recommend one for my approval.
Level 1: Look into the problem—report all the facts to me; I'll decide what to do.

Even when delegation takes place, too many supervisors fail to delegate above the first or second level of delegation. When they fail to delegate at a higher level, they are insuring themselves of constant interruptions from their subordinates. A supervisor should carefully ask herself exactly how high a level of delegation is appropriate for each task and each person.

5. *Make the Delegation.* Take care to be extremely clear to your subor-

dinate when you delegate duties. Clarify the results you intend to obtain and all the priorities involved. Of course, be certain to clarify how much authority the person has. Take the time you need to communicate all instructions carefully.

You may want to set up a chart listing each assignment you've delegated, the person to whom you've given the assignment, and the level of delegation involved. This will help you keep track of how much work you've given each subordinate and what kind of follow-up is needed for each assignment.

6. *Follow Up on the Delegated Activity.* Insist that you receive timely information. Act promptly and appropriately when anyone fails to provide this information. As we said earlier, don't insist on perfection, but do insist on results. Learn to live with the differences between the way you would have done the job and the way your subordinate did it. Don't get picky. Above all, don't call a halt to the subordinate's work by taking back the assignment. And don't forget to reward a good performance in some way.

A Note from a Successful Delegator

If you follow the points on delegation provided above, you should have minimal problems with delegation. Not only should you learn to delegate effectively—it is *mandatory* that you do.

The following note is from a successful delegator who lives in Toledo, Ohio—Carol Carrs, a 41-year-old manager of a secretarial service. She is in charge of three offices with six full-time and two part-time people (all women, by the way). She feels they are "extremely intelligent and work as hard as I do." This assessment is probably true, but her attitude toward them also makes everything run better. Here are Carol's comments on delegation:

> I delegate responsibility when they are first hired, and as they climb up the ladder in responsibility, they get more and more to do—meaning parts of my job get put onto them. So now I am overseer of the three offices, but I am always there for questions and problem solving.
>
> When I was first put in charge of only two offices, I was literally doing everything myself—which lasted exactly one month. I then started to break my job down into modules—and had the people I work with learn the modules with me. I gave them the responsibility, but I also gave them the recognition. In other words, I rewarded for jobs that management would not normally reward *me* for had I still been doing them. Not necessarily monetary rewards, but recognition, words of praise, small contests where everyone could win something; and frequently employee appraisals are rewarded with small bottles of wine, champagne, lunches, and so forth

that we all attend—and we get a temporary person to man the office while we are away.

I delegate, yes, but I take responsibility when they make mistakes with customers or the home office. I have always told them—and you can ask any one of them—that if I am away and they have to make a decision, whether it is good or bad, I have nothing to say: I wasn't there, and they did the very best they could.

Yes, I sometimes am annoyed with the decision—but I shrug and go on to something else. I have a great deal of confidence in my [subordinate] supervisors, and I share my happiness, my sadness, and my anger equally with all of them. They all know where they stand with me; their performance appraisals are never any surprise to them.

Carol is good to herself and good to work for. She provides an excellent example of effective delegation. By the way, her offices make lots of money, and everyone involved achieves rapid promotions. It shows what a confident person with good delegation skills can do.

Delegation is a key to management success. Learn to delegate as an important new behavior that will get you where you want to go!

MEET DEADLINES

Whatever you do, get in the habit of turning work in on time. Tardiness signals a lack of control, an unconcern, a lack of ability. Deadlines are crucial and continuous in the business world. Again, women have a double problem because people particularly notice their tardiness. Of course, men are frequently tardy, too, but women have the reputation for being so.

Meet those deadlines! If you have something to say about it, try to set deadlines that are realistic. Develop a time consciousness and learn to run with time efficiency. Remember the Pareto principle described in Chapter 3—80 percent of the value is accounted for by 20 percent of the items; the remaining 20 percent of the value is accounted for by the remaining 80 percent of the items. Learn to look for the critical 20 percent when you're shooting for a deadline. Concentrate your efforts on that 20 percent. Finish it up and call it good. Move on. A 100 percent effort will be required on only a few occasions. Experience will teach you when you have these occasions, but you will get nowhere trying to give 100 percent at all times.

Don't let the drive for perfection kill you. Many women point out that perfectionism is a real habit with them; actually, it is a dangerous remnant from a time when we didn't have all that much to do—so we could afford to be perfect. Today, perfectionism takes too much time. True, in many cases, a woman "has to be twice as good as a man to go half as far." When you are uptight about that phrase, remember the rest of the sentence: "fortunately, that's not too difficult." Both halves of this sentence are true— and both false; but if you buy the first half, you must take the second half (and believe it) if you're planning to enjoy peace of mind.

When you're concerned about meeting deadlines, remember to focus on your objectives, not your activities. What, exactly, do you need to accomplish? No one really cares whether you're busy all the time and are really working hard; your supervisors want results. If you can get the desired results in one hour, that's fine. If you can't get the results in ten hours, that's not so fine, no matter whether you spent ten hours on it or not. Know which activities count and which activities do not.

The ability to meet deadlines depends on the frequent use of that handy little power-packed word: *no!* Learn to use it with style. Of course, this doesn't mean you turn callous and negative to everything that's suggested to you. It simply means you evaluate the requests made of you and make a judgment. You realize that, with limited time, when you say yes to one activity, you, by definition, say no to another. What are you saying no to when you're busy saying yes to activities you believe are unimportant?

Learning to use the word *no* more effectively will also help you be a more reliable person. How's that? Look at the following example:

Say	*Do*
1. Yes	Yes
2. No	No
3. Yes	No
4. No	Yes

What you say as compared with what you do determines your yes/no reliability rating. If, for example, you say yes and you mean yes, you are a reliable person who will get the job done. You are also a reliable person if you say no and you mean no.

If, however, you say yes, and your actions indicate you meant no, you will gain a justly deserved reputation for being unreliable. This often happens when a person says yes to everything. And if you say no when everyone knows you mean yes, anything can—and will—be given to you.

Which of the four situations is most common to you? Try to identify yourself. Realize that if you frequently accept more than you can handle, you probably fall into category 3. You will tend to gain a reputation for being unreliable—that is, not doing what you say you will do. At least you will frequently have the problem of missing deadlines—a sure sign you're either accepting too much or are totally lacking in knowledge of time control.

Start early when you have a deadline. Plan the steps you'll need to fulfill your obligation on time. Plan carefully by the year, the quarter, the month, the week, and the day. Start early in the day, too. You'll get more done, and what you get accomplished will serve as fuel for further accomplishments.

Deadlines are an important part of the schedule-oriented business system. Other people depend on the work you do. If you're late, you set off a negative chain reaction that makes many others late. Once you develop this reputation, it's very difficult to overcome it. Be on time; turn in those projects on or before the day they are due.

THE FEMALE MANAGERIAL ROLE—YOU'RE IT!

Although the number of female managers is increasing, the idea of a woman as the manager is considered a new concept. Many people who theoretically believe it's a fair idea to have women in management will react negatively when it happens to them. It will be many years before a lot of people feel as comfortable working for a woman as for a man. It is not always clear to the manager herself or to her subordinates exactly how this role should be handled. Therefore, when you reach the management ranks, *you* define the role. You are setting a powerful example and making a strong statement. Your success or failure affects all women managers your subordinates will ever have. It's a big responsibility.

Remember, first of all, that your aim should be to gain respect, not love, in your role as a manager. Don't mother your subordinates; manage them with confidence, compassion, and care. Don't play games, but meet your challenges head on. This takes self-confidence—a trait not easily acquired by males or females but a trait the successful managers have in abundance. You must believe in yourself before anyone else will believe in you.

To truly gain a leadership role, you must *act* your position. Many women make the mistake of acting like clock-punchers when they have been promoted beyond that point. They're frequently afraid to act bossy or pushy, and they bend over backward to show they're still "one of the girls." This is dangerous to their careers and confusing to their subordinates. Of course, they can be friendly, but their job is to be a manager first and a friend second—not the reverse.

Women must learn to feel comfortable with differential rewards. No, everything is not equal, and everyone doesn't have equal skills and opportunities. Some people will make more than others; some will make less. There are different rewards for different people. Along with the laws of competition, that's how it works.

Accept the success you achieve without guilt pangs. You are not a failure as a woman because you are successful in business, although some women feel they are. It's part of the price we pay for being different from the traditional female model. In another generation, in another time, our daughters won't feel uncomfortable. Many of us still will.

It's crucial that women learn to use their special sensitivity to understand those below and above them. I don't believe this is a sexist statement, although some will think it is. People of any size, shape, color (or sex) who have been in a subordinate position to a dominant class have learned to read signals carefully. Their very life frequently depends upon it. Women, therefore, also have a well-known special sensitivity to people that can help them when they're on top as well as when they're not on top. This sensitivity can be very useful in gaining employee respect and adherence to certain policies. It can also be used to create a more pleasant work environment, for a boss who understands is better to work for than a boss who doesn't!

As part of understanding people, realize that those who are subordinate to you can do without constant reminders of your successes. Don't brag about your accomplishments. Take personal joy in your successes but realize that many people aren't truly glad for you when you advance. You're lucky when a few people are on your side and happy for you. Learn to rely on these friends and share your joys only with them. These friends may only be family members, but then again, many family members are often less than pleased over your accomplishments. Siblings may still carry wounds of competition from your earlier years, and your spouse may be working through his own hang-ups regarding your being successful (particularly if he thinks you're more successful than he). Use your sensitivity along with the rule "Win without bragging; lose without complaining," and you should be as safe as you can be.

Remember to respect all people, no matter what their rank. Keep the size of your head in check. All people are worth something, no matter what function they perform around your shop.

The worth of all people in the office was brought vividly to our attention in 1971–72, when my husband and I were working with an institute in Copenhagen, Denmark. The institute was associated with a university. Various levels of help were employed: a director, several researchers, cooks, research assistants, janitors, secretaries, telephone operators, and so on. Of course, different levels of employment brought different levels of status and money. However, there was an interesting difference in this institute. Everyone ate together in a common dining room, *and* everyone voted on who became a permanent member of the institute. This meant the cooks and janitors got a "yea" or "nay" vote over the tenured professors. This provided a very interesting twist to the relationships in the hierarchy. It has long served as a reminder to me that all people are important in any organization. Although most janitors don't have a direct say over your employment, their indirect effect can be very important. Treating all persons in a way that is respectful of their personal dignity can only serve your cause in the long run. Most importantly, the way you treat others speaks strongly of your own worth.

The balance between respecting all persons and letting everyone walk all over you is a very delicate one. Many people easily slip in one direction or another. This is part of why success is so difficult to attain: It is made up of one difficult balancing act built upon another. There are just no easy answers.

With practice, confidence, and effort, however, this balance can be achieved. By paying attention to the crucial points made in this chapter, you will be meeting directly and squarely the problems many women face. Learning your job as outlined in the job description is only a part of the battle, and it may very well be the smaller part. The major part of the question is wound around interpersonal issues—issues that can make or break you.

Everyone has doubts; the successful people learn to live with their doubts and handle them. Handle yours. Learn to feel and live the new attitudes and behaviors necessary to get you where you want to go, while keeping a finger on important human feelings, needs, and potential.

PART III
ON THE HOME FRONT

6

THE HOME
OR
And the walls came tumbling down

The home is a major source of problems for many working women. A woman has a home, even if she doesn't have a family, and most women feel very pressured by the demands of that home. Even women living alone (contrary to the belief of many women with children) find they suffer from household pressures. In fact, the only group of women I talked to concerning career/home conflicts who didn't have a problem with the home were those women living in their parents' home, with mom in charge of traditional household duties. (There are more of them than you might think!)

Home is supposed to be a place where you can rest from the day's toils. It's supposed to be a haven from the rest of the world, a place where you can regroup and regain your energies to meet the world once again tomorrow.

Traditionally it *was* this resting place—for the man who returned from his labors. It has seldom been much of a resting place for the housewife whom the phrase maker had in mind when he coined the saying, "A woman's work is never done!" Now that women are out in the world of paid employment, too, they need a resting place more than ever. But when they return from putting in their eight to nine hours, they find their second (or is it their first?) job still waiting for them.

Housework is usually the first topic mentioned when a woman is asked about her biggest at-home time problem. When I first talked to Hattie Upman, a 26-year-old credit union administrative assistant who has a year-old son, about her biggest at-home pressures, she stated:

I just don't have time to get all my housecleaning done *and* have time for myself. This often frustrates me, and I get nervous when things just don't get finished.

When I asked Hattie if she could identify what made her become uptight about housework, she got somewhat defensive:

Though I am *not* a compulsive house cleaner, I do feel certain chores must be done for me to feel comfortable in my home. This is basically keeping the house "picked up." Generally, I have little problem with this, but if this work is not done, I find I cannot relax, because it's always nagging at the back of my mind. I realize this stems from the way I was raised, but it is very difficult to let go of that training.

Hattie is caught in the Donna Reed syndrome. Remember her? On *The Donna Reed Show* during the 1950s, Donna was a housewife married to Dr. Alex Stone. She had two children, a boy and a girl, who were generally perfect. Donna always wore earrings, a belted dress, stockings, high heels, and a smile. She floated around her sparkling clean home.

"Donna" is still in our brains. Even women as young as 26-year-old Hattie have mental pictures that haunt them. Besides the "Donna" images to live up to, most women have mothers and grandmothers to please, even though many wouldn't admit the pressure. We can't blame our mothers and grandmothers totally, however, for we, ourselves, are adults and merely feel obliged to carry on in their time-honored tradition.

Habits cause most of the pressure. These habits were established early in our lives, as we watched our mothers; early in our independent years, when we had a small apartment and no one to mess it up; or early in our marriages, when we had little to do and were eager to play the role.

The "pot roast" story makes a good point about housekeeping habits:

Once upon a time, a young husband narued Jim watched his bride, Sue, as she prepared dinner. Sue was cooking a pot roast. Before she put the meat in the roaster, however, she cut two inches off each end.

"Why did you cut off the ends?" Jim asked her curiously.

"Because mom always did it that way," was Sue's explanation.

The next Sunday at his mother-in-law's home, as luck would have it, pot roast was again on the menu. Jim watched his mother-in-law go through the same routine, cutting the ends of the pot roast off before placing it in the roasting pan.

"Why did you cut off the ends?" Jim asked her curiously.

"Because my mother always did it that way," replied Sue's mother.

By now, Jim's curiosity was aroused. He decided to get to the bottom of this mystery and searched the house until he found grandma, sitting quietly in her room reading the Sunday paper.

"Grandma," he began, "I have to ask you something. Sue and her mother both cut off the ends of their pot roasts before cooking them. Both of them say they do it because that's the way you did it. Why'd you do it that way?"

"That's easy, Jimmy," grandma replied. "My pot was too small!"

How many "pot roasts" are there in your life? I have a feeling we all have many of them. We seldom question our habits; it's easier to continue doing our work the way it's always been done. When we work outside the home, however, these habits can be killers, as many women are finding out.

The tradition of the spotless household is only one culprit; television and other media continually bombard us with the virtues of the "Mr. Clean" home. Cleaning products are part of a multimillion-dollar industry. The manufacturers, of course, are out to sell us what they can, and who can blame them? They're in the business to make a profit. It's up to us to realize that part of that business involves convincing all of us that we need their products—to make our homes clean!

The main point here is that "The House" is not a place but a state of mind. Repeat: "The House" is a state of mind. The standards you set for cleanliness are up to you and no one else. Few children have died because they lived in a dirty house, so why all the fuss?

The question you have to ask yourself is how much you have been paying for the dream (seldom the reality) of a perfect house. Has it cost you your relationship with your children, your hobbies, your *joie de vivre*, your sanity? Has it cost you your freedom because you always have chores hanging over your head? If you've paid this price, is it worth it? Would the price of a housekeeper actually be cheaper?

If you honestly consider the true cost of your clean-house mania, you may rethink your housekeeping standards. When you take the time to sit down and review the important activities you must give up for the sake of your personal house beautiful, you may come to the same conclusions as May:

I used to be an immaculate housekeeper, but you know, anymore I just don't care. I've been to lots of my friends' funerals, and never once has the minister mentioned that she kept a clean house!

May hits the nail on the head: What's it all ultimately worth, anyway?

Many women equate being a good housekeeper with being a good wife and mother. Of course, there is *some* relationship, but the two are *not* the same thing. *Traditionally*, "housewife" and "wife/mother" were thought to be the same role. But we all know women who are excellent wives and mothers but terrible housekeepers; conversely, we all know terrible wives and mothers who are wonderful housekeepers. This point became obvious to me one day when a friend of mine told me over coffee that she could barely remember her mother from her childhood. "Oh, mom was always around, but she was always cooking, cleaning, ironing, washing, and so on. And she was always tired."

This mother probably loved her children very much, but I'm certain she'd want to turn back the clock if she could hear her daughter's sad comment. Unfortunately, it's likely her husband would have similar memories; in fact, housecleaning chores are probably the only memory the woman herself has of her own life! Yet there is much more—if only we can escape the prison we've put ourselves in. We *can* unlock the door.

GOALS OF THE HOME

What is the goal of the home? For most families, it is this: to provide a living and resting place that will enhance the happiness and effectiveness of the family members. This goal isn't as tangible as most industrial goals, but it is worthwhile. When we consider this goal definition, we place the home in a supportive role instead of the dominant role. The house is there to serve the family; the family is not there to serve and pay homage to the house. Any household activities that get in the way of family happiness, harmony, and effectiveness should be critically questioned.

No, I'm not advocating living in a pigpen. I'm merely suggesting that you question your standards, question your motives, and question the purpose they serve. As many a mother has learned, her relationship with her child can be reduced to a constant battle over cleaning his or her bedroom. Is that special relationship worth it?

Occasionally I let the Donna Reed syndrome slip back into my head. One day I found myself nagging my five-year-old daughter to pick up the mess in her room. There was a tea party on the floor to the left of me, a doll house to the right of me, a toy typewriter on the bed, a kite in the corner, and tennis shoes in the doorway.

"Mom," she complained, "wasn't your room messy when you were a little girl?" (How do I get out of this one?)

I stood staring at her for a minute. The door to her room is next to the door to our guest room, and I could see both rooms clearly from where I stood. The guest room was perfect, sitting there comfortably with its gold and blue decor, just as I had planned. The pictures were straight. The wastebasket was clean.

"Jen," I said, "come here." My husband approached us to listen in on our conversation. "Which of the two rooms do you think mommy thinks looks the best?"

"Oh, that's easy, mom," was her quick answer. "You like that neat guest room."

I got a hug from my husband on this one; he caught the tears in my eyes, although Jenny didn't.

"No, sweetheart," I answered, "I like *your* room best! It looks like so much more fun! Let's play office with your dolls!"

Some future year, her room will be perfectly neat, too. I'm glad it will be filled with a lot of happy memories as a worn-out doll silently observes the uncluttered domain.

Even if I had no children, I would still ask myself what a perfectly clean home has cost *me*. What personal dreams went unfulfilled because I spent so much time cleaning? A true awareness of how precious—and how limited—time is can be very helpful when you're trying to determine cost.

M.E.D.

After you have successfully adjusted your household ambitions to your busy reality, how do you go about choosing the work that still must be done? You can decide what is important and necessary for you, personally, with the help of a handy little system known as "M.E.D."

"M.E.D." are my husband's initials, and it gives me particular joy to use them in connection with this topic. Merrill has been one of the nation's leading time-management consultants for over ten years, so it's appropriate that his initials comfortably cover "minimize," "eliminate," and "delegate."

Ask yourself which household tasks you can minimize. The house should be cleaned, but does it have to be cleaned every day? In fact (horrors!), does it have to be cleaned every week? Again, you and you alone are left to decide how much of your time and money you want to exchange for a clean house.

The family members must eat to maintain their health, but fortunately the healthiest food is also some of the easiest to prepare. A breakfast of whole-grain cereal, milk, and fruit is next to no work at all and is far healthier than fried eggs, bacon, and white toast. The same principle applies to other meals and snacks.

Clothes still must be cleaned, but with an automatic washer and dryer, they can be cleaned almost effortlessly, as you walk by the machine on the way out the door. If you purchase only no-iron clothes and take them out of the dryer as soon as it stops, you can forget where your iron is stored.

Towels and underwear, of course, can be folded during the evening news or while you and your son chat about the day's events (get him to help!).

"Deep" cleaning is a different problem, but many women happily report they have ignored deep cleaning for years! The choice here, of course, is to hire it done every five years or so—or turn it into a big family Saturday morning event, complete with an ordered-out pizza break for lunch.

The philosophy behind all this is called "the bare basics approach," and it's very simple: Ask yourself what are the absolutely minimal tasks that must be performed for your family to stay alive and function happily. Take it from there. When you wave the "bare basics" wand over your household, you'll be surprised at the freedom you'll discover. Most of the things you used to think were necessary really aren't after all.

Once you start thinking of the jobs you can minimize, go a step further and see what burdens you can eliminate altogether. Honestly, throw them out! The world won't fall apart. Some women would find this absolutely impossible to do; they are so habituated to performing certain jobs as soon as they walk in the door, as soon as they get up in the morning, or as soon as dinner is finished, that they'd fail to recognize a task that could be questioned. If you need help, consider these radical ideas:

1. Lose your iron. You honestly haven't needed it in the last ten years.
2. Put your baking pans in a garage sale or at least far removed from everyday life. The word is that you don't need to bake anymore. Excellent bakery products are now available for purchase in stores and restaurants. If you *love* to bake, that's a different story; then it's a hobby, not a necessity.
3. Don't polish silverware. If you must keep it, save it to pass to future generations as an heirloom. Buy pewter or stainless for everyday use.
4. Don't dust all the pictures and figurines. Build or buy a glass display case to cover them.

I meant to have a longer list of suggestions, but there are so many chores I've ignored for so many years, I can no longer recall what they are. We live happily and healthily with so little housework on anyone's part (I have a cleaning lady only twice a month) that I sometimes honestly wonder what housewives do all day.

Some women, of course, spend 20 hours a day, 7 days a week, cleaning their house; and of course, this is their right. Many of them say, "I like a *clean* house." This may be true, but it's also likely they've failed to identify anything truly important in their lives and fill the void with busywork. They clean house because that's all there is to do (in addition to hollering at their families for messing it up!).

Once you've carefully identified all the tasks you can either minimize or eliminate, delegate the remaining ones. If you can afford it, you might want to hire some of it done. If you can't afford it, you're stuck with the family at hand, but don't overlook the possibilities here. Of course, the more children you have, the more there is to do; *but* the more children you have, the more *help* you have! This help should include far more than making their own beds in the morning. Their responsibility should increase rapidly with age, but even the very young ones can do their share.

My children know, without a doubt, that there is no servant living in this house! Everyone must do his or her share. My 16-year-old son, Steve, for example, never even *thinks* of asking me to do his laundry; he's done his own since he was 11. His sister, Susan, also started doing her own laundry when she turned 11, and it works so well that 5-year-old Jennifer will be doing her own as soon as she can reach the dial on the machine. At 4 years old, she was already in charge of folding towels, washcloths, underwear, and pillowcases. She could also sort clothes and put fresh pillowcases on the pillows. More will be said about children in a later chapter, but the main point here is: The more children, the more help. And the earlier you get to them, the better.

In most families, the woman is still the household manager. As household managers, the most successful women are those who can truly take charge of the tasks. Just as with an office manager, it is her job to *manage*, not to do it all, unless she is the only one in the house. Just as it is an office manager's job to develop her subordinates to perform the necessary tasks, it is the home manager's job to develop her "subordinates" in the necessities of living. That means learning to take care of themselves, not being taken care of by mother.

Our job as mothers is to raise our children to be independent, not dependent. We have failed if we have not done this. Independence takes tough love, not "smother" love. The women who wait on their children, as a servant waits on her master, have instilled all the wrong values and skills in their offspring. The sorry losers are the children as well as the mother. The mother usually earns sass and disdain instead of love and respect for her efforts. She is left to cry, "And after all I've done for you!"

Of course, I believe the man of the house should carry his share of household duties. Again, the earlier you get to him in your life together, the better chance you have to get him to cooperate. Day One may already be too late if he had a mother who waited on him hand and foot when he was young (although some ambitious young women have done wonders with formerly pampered husbands)! I honestly don't blame men for dragging their feet when it comes to jumping in and sharing household duties. I wouldn't easily give up being waited on—not if I had a choice. Many men have changed, however, and met the challenge of living with a woman who shares the income-producing responsibilities. These men have come to enjoy having some help on the financial end and realize the inequities of expecting the women to perform all the at-home tasks as well as their out-of-home tasks.

Not all men are this flexible, however. Some adamantly refuse to co-operate. Some women have fought this battle, without success, for years. They are constantly angry and displeased; their antagonism has ruined their entire relationship. I know of one household where a pair of men's socks is rotting under the kitchen table. Neither the man nor the woman of the house will pick them up. He claims it's her job to pick them up, and she claims they're his socks! This scenario is played out, in one form or another, every day, all over the country!

When faced with this conflict, there is obviously more at issue than a pair of socks on the kitchen floor! Many bitter feelings, many hurts, and many insecurities are lying there along with that old pair of socks. How do you move off dead center when your personal identity is at stake?

I believe the same rule that applies to stubborn children applies to stubborn husbands. What price are you willing to pay to win your point? Are you willing to become a constant nag? Are you willing to walk around with hurt feelings in an environment as thick as pea soup? Are you willing to sacrifice any chance of happiness in your marriage?

Marriage is made of compromises, but we all feel we shouldn't be the one to give in all the time. The other party should give in once in a while. All this is true. But what if your "better half" will never give in, especially on this issue?

You have few choices. The first choice is to constantly fight about it. This, of course, is no fun and a no-win situation. The second choice is to divorce him, but this is a no-win alternative, too, and you would probably lose a lot more than you would gain. The third choice is to pick up those darn socks, losing the little battle—but being smart enough to win the war!

How do you win the war when you just gave in? You are obviously the more mature one, the one willing to bend when bending is necessary. But now that you have the upper hand, use it. Begin to develop that self-confidence about yourself that thrives on inner strength instead of petty issues. The more you learn to focus on other possibilities in your life, the smaller a pair of socks (and what it represents) becomes. If a pair of socks is all that's standing between you and the loss of your human dignity, then of course, the issue is crucial. But if you've just completed a successful political campaign, performed *Rhapsody in Blue* on the piano for an appre-ciative crowd of 500, or closed the deal on an important contract, you can pick up the socks on the way to the refrigerator and toss them in the chute on the way to the bedroom without even noticing! You *can* handle the small stuff without thinking about it—so don't think about it—don't focus on it—don't get angry about it. Honestly don't get angry about it. *You're* the one who suffers with ulcers when you get angry, not him. He'll forget about it. Learn not to let it bug you. Just continue to develop your independence in other fields, and you'll begin to feel better and better about yourself.

He'll notice, too, and there's a good chance you'll see some changes. Who knows, you may even notice him picking up socks some day. Miracles do happen. But gloating isn't called for if he does, because you will both have progressed beyond it. Neither of you will need to make a big deal of such trite matters. You will have outgrown such silliness, and so will he. Best of all, you'll both be winners, growing together.

The secret of handling the household chores is learning to take control. Develop a realistic attitude about your home and the activities required to run it. Realize that the house is your servant, not vice versa. Learn to minimize, eliminate, and delegate the jobs necessary to make it a happy and healthy place to live.

BASIC FUNCTION ROOMS

Certain rooms of the house are more subject to conflict and discord because they are basic function rooms. These are the rooms where you and everyone else in the house are involved in the basic functions of living. The bathroom and the kitchen are the leading basic function rooms.

More bad air (excuse the pun) has developed over the rights in the bathroom than over any other room in the house. Marriages have dissolved because of elbowing in the bathroom. Siblings have been known to pull each other's hair out because of bathroom battles. Carpenters have become rich from repairing bathroom door frames demolished as five people fought to go through the opening at once. Bathrooms! Ideally, everyone should own his or her own, but what if this is impossible?

If you have the chance, build in or buy as many bathrooms as possible. Two per house is never too many, and three is quite necessary for any family of five or more. Teenagers are fabled bathroom hogs; it's part of their personality, and a lot of discord can be saved during these trying years if there are adequate bathroom facilities.

If you're stuck with something less than adequate facilities (one woman wrote me that she had six teenagers, her husband and herself, and one grandparent—on one bathroom!), some privacy and order must be maintained; this will happen only through planning.

If the storage space is available, everyone will be happier if he or she has a place to keep personal toiletries. A drawer or shelf will do nicely.

A friend of mine installed this system and has made peace with her 17-year-old son for the first time in five years. Sometimes he remembers to put the toothpaste cap on, and sometimes he doesn't. Sometimes he remembers to put the toothpaste and his toothbrush away, and sometimes he doesn't. Sometimes he forgets to put his pimple medication, shaving lotion, and hair dryer away, and sometimes he doesn't. So, as an alternative to nagging someone who hears only 10 percent of the time anyway, she cleaned out the washcloth drawer and made it *his* drawer. She awarded him his own private tube of toothpaste.

Now, she finds, it's more likely he'll put his supplies away; but if he doesn't, she does it without complaints. No irritation and no time involved. She's developed a two-second-swing that will land it all in the opened drawer with one quick movement. She does it without a second thought on her way to the shower. At least the issue is out of the way, and she doesn't have to bring it up when he's eager to talk about his friend on drugs or his progressing sex life! Again, a matter of priorities.

If there's not enough drawer or shelf space for everyone to have a personal spot, move to the dormitory technique. Buy everyone an inexpensive plastic carrier and let each person develop a private bathroom kit. Store the bathroom kits in the bedroom closets or in some place where space isn't as limited.

Most families with too few bathrooms have developed a morning bathroom routine. George gets up at 5:30 to get in the bathroom. When he's finished, he knocks on Gail's door (around 6:00), and she has her turn. Peggy and Clair follow at 6:30 and 7:00 A.M. Some households have established shower time limits to stretch scarce hot water. Some have convinced or bribed two or three household members to transfer some of their bathroom routine to the evening hours, with the attractive incentive of a more leisurely experience. Larger bedroom mirrors and better bedroom lighting have also helped cut down early-morning confusion, as hair and faces can be prepared to meet the day somewhere other than the bathroom. Anything that works is worth a try when it comes to this popular facility—one of the most explosive rooms in the house.

The kitchen is another basic function room, for eating is definitely basic. Unlike bathroom activities, however, which should be a more private matter, kitchen activities can be fun and social as well as necessary. Like a scene from a Grandma Moses painting, the kitchen should be a happy, warm place, full of chatter and sharing. Yes, meals must be cooked, but when everyone works together, cooking can be a joy instead of a chore.

Anyone who eats should get to share in preparing and cleanup on a regular basis. Again, unless you've paid one, there's no servant in the house. The same woman who wrote that she had a husband, a mother, and six teenagers living in her single-bathroom home also reported that she did all the cooking and cleanup. She must be suffering from a real martyr complex. She is also missing a lot of intimacy with her family and building up a lot of resentment and guilt instead.

Kitchen duties can be delegated by "department." With the department system, there's a main-course person, a salad person, a vegetable person, a table-setting person, a cleanup person, a dish washer, and a dish put-away person. Sometimes these jobs are combined. One household of three had two job classifications: preparer and cleaner. Every third night, you got an evening off.

The objective is sharing the job, and fortunately, when the job is preparing meals, a lot of good communication can be enjoyed as well. I'll never forget the first time we turned on soft classical music in the background while we fixed dinner as a family. Candlelight with dinner seemed to follow naturally. And after a pleasant candlelight dinner, no one complained about staying for the wind-down activities of cleaning up.

The saying goes: "When you get a lemon, make lemonade." We can modify this to point out that, although cooking can be a chore, it can be turned into something more—such as a time for caring and sharing. Cooperation comes as everyone begins to benefit from the resulting communication.

There is another basic function place that most people forget about. The basic function performed here is being alone. A private place is crucially important for all people, but particularly for those who both enjoy and suffer from a hectic, active life. Social interaction with friends and family is essential, but a time for retreat into your own realm is also vital to maintaining your stability and direction.

Everyone should have a private place. Children have long enjoyed the thought that they needed their own room, their own tree house, their own hole, or their own cave. Men have often enjoyed the luxury of a home office or workshop. But for years, women have had no place to call their own except their underwear drawer. Unfortunately, you can't crawl into it. Perhaps this is the reason women have been known to lock themselves in the bathroom for hours at a time. It is frequently the only place they can hide to get away from it all for a while.

Find a private spot and help other household members find theirs. If two of your children share a room, they usually belligerently split it down the middle, threatening to kill anyone who crosses over into their territory.

Look for possibilities for yourself. An extra bedroom is obvious. A large closet is not so obvious, but it's also a good choice, and you probably don't need all the things you've stored in there anyway. (Have a garage sale or call Goodwill.) The basement offers many possibilities. You can get as elaborate or as simple as you choose with the design. Just find your own place. Retreat there whenever you need revitalizing.

THE ROUTINE TRACK

There are thousands of household hints books, columns, articles, and pamphlets that tell you 1,001 different ways to do things faster and better in the home. Check these out and choose the methods that appeal to you.* But the real secret of getting the important tasks done centers on the ideas presented here. Determine a realistic objective. Minimize, eliminate, and delegate whatever time-consuming tasks you can. Organize the remaining tasks through scheduling your routine operation. Make this your household motto: If it's necessary, put it on the routine track. Here's how you do it:

1. What activities must be done every two to three years? Write them on December 31 in "off" years and assign these tasks to a particular month during the "on" years.
2. What activities must be done once a year? Dental checkups? Physicals? Washing the outside of the windows? Set a specific time for these events. Many people routinely use their birthday as a signal for their personal yearly "tune-up." Birthdays are a good, private day to take inventory of yourself—your physical self as well as your inner self. What are your goals? Where are you going?
3. What activities must be done each month? Check the oil? Tires? Pay bills? Write them in.

Weekly and daily routines become true habit and run themselves. If you develop the habit of watering the plants each Tuesday, you'll soon find you actually can't go to bed unless you have given the ivy its scheduled shower. Use these habits to avoid minor disasters that upset your life.

This approach may sound dull and boring to some people. It is a little boring, like many necessary activities of life. But by relegating these jobs

* A free booklet entitled "Quick Tips for a Busy Day" is loaded with proven ideas on general time management, organization, and household efficiency. I've been collecting these time-saving tips for years and would like to share them with you. To get your free copy, send a self-addressed, stamped envelope to Quick Tips for a Busy Day, Time Management Center, 7612 Florissant Road, St. Louis, MO 63121.

to a routine, you've taken care of them without focusing on them. They get done, but they don't interrupt the other parts of your life that you think are more important. You have freed yourself from mundane tasks by giving them to your unconscious, your routine.

The home should mean peace. It should be a haven of contentment and support. But it takes a special attitude, approach, and effort to get it to function in the proper, beneficial way. The details of repairing and cleaning it should not become the main focus; when this happens, we have another case of the tail wagging the dog.

Many of us are still dreaming of a self-cleaning house. If they've done it with ovens, why not houses? Well, someone is trying. Frances Gabe, a grandmother from Oregon, is working on just that. "My dream is to have self-cleaning houses the world over," she claims. As of this writing, Mrs. Gabe has 68 laborsaving devices pending patents. Her ideas include a fireplace with a back door through which ashes are flushed away, a whirlpool-like bathtub that squirts a degreaser and then cleans itself, a cupboard that doubles as a dishwasher, and a clothes-freshener closet that launders garments and leaves them to drip dry on the hanger. Go to it, Mrs. Gabe! We all love you!

In the meantime, minimize, eliminate, delegate, and routinize. Decide what's important and forget the rest. Discover the activities that are really meaningful to your life and develop your skills and interests in other areas. Once you honestly know what to do with your time—once you know and act on what makes you feel excited and alive—household chores will have a new meaning. "The House" will comfortably become a home, a nesting place kept to soothe its weary inhabitants.

7

THE OTHER HALF

OR

It's so nice to have a man around the house

When we say "I do," few of us realize what we're saying "I do" to. Whether we say "I do" to a marriage we anticipate will last for a lifetime or to a live-in arrangement we plan to try for an indefinite period, we have no way of knowing what the future will hold; nor do we anticipate the difficult trials that will surely come.

Twenty years ago, the word *mate* meant either a husband or a wife. The fact that today *mate* can refer to someone other than the legal spouse is indicative of just how much our society and our relationship with the opposite sex have changed during the past few years. An unmarried mate is accepted in many circles today. This chapter, however, primarily deals with the version of mating known as marriage.

For better or worse, the very foundation of what marriage has always meant was changed when women began moving into the workforce. No one is defending the traditional mold (there was a lot wrong with it), but it at least defined the way marriage "should" be. A radical change of any sort was bound to have drastic ramifications and cause major adjustments. Women working was just that sort of change.

FINANCIAL INDEPENDENCE

The most earthshaking change that occurred when women began working was that they became financially independent of their husbands. The woman no longer needed a man to feed her, clothe her, or in any way financially support her. The institution of marriage lost an important component—that of financial dependency on the part of the woman. It meant a woman no longer had to put up with actions and attitudes on the part of the husband that she found intolerable simply because she had nowhere else to turn. It meant she had earned the right to have a say in the decisions of the marriage—that she wanted the authority in the home to go along with the power she had found in the marketplace.

The female wage earner also became a real bonus to the man who readily adjusted to a more powerful wife. No longer must that man be the sole means of survival for the family. He had true help. This financial power gave many women the confidence they needed to also help their husbands with all the major decisions that affected their lives. A man no longer had to make all those life/death decisions (which affected him, his wife, and his children) alone.

Whatever men regarded as the pluses and minuses when their wives found employment outside the home, however, many men were left with the insecurity of a threatening question: "If she doesn't need me to survive, will she keep me?"

It's a very interesting question, indeed. In the old days, women had no choice. But today, why should women bother with marriage when there's no real need? Why should they voluntarily put themselves in a state of subordination, or at least in a role where they must fight to keep their sense of self, no matter how modern the man they choose might be?

The answer to "Will she keep me?" has been "no!" in many cases. Divorce has become more prevalent as women decide they want completely out of their traditional role. Some women have chosen to skip marriage altogether and concentrate on their careers. Many have chosen to bear children out of wedlock and raise them alone or adopt children as a single parent rather than put up with the demands of a man. Somewhere, some men must have been hurt by these decisions, but if such feelings were that intense in these women, the scorned men were fortunate *not* to have married them.

In many more cases, however, women have opted *for* having a man around, even if he isn't needed for financial security. Here, some working women offer interesting comments on why a husband is worth it:

A husband is a warm haven from the outside world. He's another pair of hands with the children. And he helps me avoid the appearance of being "on the make" in the business world.

My husband has dinner ready on weeknights. He helps with the dishes. He helps with the weekend cleaning of the house.

Husbands help you, as an individual, keep it all together. If things go bad at work, you can come home, talk it out, get it off your chest, and feel better, even if you haven't got the problem solved just yet. My husband helps me see what perspective I should put things in, many times before I ever realize just what those things are.

While independence is something that we women are desperately striving for, I believe that we must not undermine the basic instinctual need for male/female bonding. If my back will not survive the years of work I must perform, I know my mind shall, so I have a real faith in myself to take care of myself. That (the need of being taken care of) is not the instinctual need I speak of. I do not desire a man for a financial support. Rather it is a complementary, contra-female emotional support which I look for. It's a bonding of female/male spirits which allows for this support system to develop.

The "contra-female" perspective is one of the most valid reasons going to keep a man around. A man's presence provides a balanced sense of "otherness" in our lives that allows us to reflect, to see an issue from a distinct, yet interested perspective. The husband keeps us from living a totally narcissistic life. He makes demands on us yet observes the world from a different viewpoint. When the marriage is a good match, a man and a woman are part of a complementary team. When they work together, they can present the best of all fronts against a frequently hostile environment.

SEMILIBERATION

A lot of the problems in two-career marriages develop because most of us are semiliberated. We're neither from the traditional mold nor from the modern school that insists men and women can and should be equal in all things. The problematic word here is *equal*. Pure equality is technically impossible, for the work and rewards of marriage are not totally measurable. Therefore, the work and contribution of each partner are left to subjective judgment. Who can say whether or not mowing the lawn is more or less important than washing the windows? Who can say whether or not cooking dinner is worth one or two turns at changing the cat litter? Couples who attempt to prove they're a modern partnership by keeping exact count of who does what are headed for trouble. At some point, one party or the other is bound to call "foul!" with the ensuing argument finding both parties the losers.

Traditional expectations are so inbred in most of us that marriage partners of both sexes tend to follow the role model set by their parents. Women generally believe they have the most to gain by calling for a fair splitting of the workload, because half the total job looks a lot easier than doing it all.

Most men, on the other hand, drag their feet on the question of sharing the work, because it's always easier to let someone else do it. Traditions die hard. Then, too, there's such a great difference in men. Some men feel that doing "woman's work" is degrading; some men also feel offended if their wives are personally successful. Some are more secure than others, thus less threatened by successful women. The dangers that result from a threatened husband are far more critical than the issue of who dusts the piano.

A large number of women reported husbands who were threatened by their success in the business world. Some of the comments are very thought-provoking:

> He feels my job is more important than he is. Actually he is more important, but he must understand my goals and objectives and the time it takes to accomplish them. I quite often stay up late working at home after my husband has gone to bed. This does wonders to destroy a relationship. However, this is something we have to cope with.

> At first, in the beginning of my work, he was extremely jealous or threatened or both. Being a product of the early fifties, I fell right into the pattern of giving my all to husband and children. I always had a struggle within myself as to the justice or injustice of it all. Perhaps my selfish streak ran deep and lay dormant for awhile. But he stated once that he hoped I wouldn't become a success, for if I did, chances are I wouldn't need him anymore.

> My husband admits to being lazy. He doesn't seem able to see what needs doing around the house, and if he does, he doesn't do it until I finally have to mention it. I think it's a game he plays so "mother" will tell him what to do. I would say he has done little to help me, even though I have asked a number of times. He has said that since I am so successful and have everything my way (i.e., have no children yet) I can just do it myself. I have tried to sit with him in the evenings to visit, but he usually watches TV and barely hears me, so after a while I just leave him alone. I like to touch and hold him, but he usually pushes me away. He used to be tolerant of my activities, but he is no longer tolerant and wants me to be home.

> He fears I'm smarter than he is—or might be. Why he worries, I can't fathom, since our interests, intelligence, and strengths are in different areas of expertise.

Again, traditional role expectation takes its toll. Even when some husbands believe they can be happy for their wives' successes, they are put to the test when they are asked to share housework, asked to share decisions and power, and made to realize that their wives can bring home a considerable amount of money from a tough marketplace. Many men who originally thought it would be great to have double the money find themselves a little unsure if and when their wives earn more than they do. A very strong ego is called for, and as we all know, solid egos are in short supply.

Many husbands of successful women also feel alone. Their loneliness may be an outgrowth of insecurity, but it probably has a basis in fact as well. We have only so much time, and when we have a job, a home, professional activities, and kids calling for our attention, a husband can easily be left out in the cold. In a busy life, something has to give; without careful planning and priority setting, that "something" is usually the husband. Many a busy woman has complained that her man fails to cooperate. "He should be more supportive of my career needs" is frequently heard when working women get together to commiserate. It's almost ironic: The working man has made this demand of his wife for years. Now, it seems, it's woman's turn.

Changing roles is difficult for everyone. It's hard to be both dependent and independent at the same time, or even at the right time. In a two-career marriage, you're dealing with two people who are charting a new course, seeking that delicate balance between dependency and self-reliance. There is no perfect balance, and the definition of *even keel* changes from day to day.

AGE OF THE EGO

Complicating the issue of fluctuating role definitions is the push for personal development and individual gratification. The "age of the ego" demands that we seek what is best for us personally. Give-and-take becomes out of fashion in this age. When something doesn't please us, we discard it and run over it. Whatever glorifies us personally is what's best. The age of the ego has nothing but disdain for the person who subordinates his or her needs and desires to the needs of another. This, of course, spells death for a harmonious marriage, because marriage, by definition, means give-and-take.

One woman told me the age of the ego had totally passed her by. Her comment made me realize that not everyone feels the self-centeredness of the age. Unfortunately, the philosophy of self is so prevalent that most marriages are affected by it in one way or another. If either of the partners in a marriage is focused on the self, the marriage has serious difficulties. It was sad to notice that the woman who made this statement was one of the nicest people I'd ever met, but she had married young and for the next seven years played doormat for a husband who sought only his own pleasures. She had ignored, tolerated, and then cried over his activities. Finally, she walked away.

The age of the ego leaves all involved parties a little dissatisfied. Few people become the Renaissance Man or Renaissance Woman they had dreamed of being. They become disillusioned with themselves and turn their anger both inward and outward. When they turn it outward, they begin to "nag." They complain about everything in sight to the closest one in sight—usually the spouse. It's more comfortable to blame others for personal shortcomings, even when the personal goals had been set too high. If we blame someone else, we at least are left with the comfort of feeling that we could have succeeded, if only we hadn't had the albatross around our neck. "If only Fred had been more supportive" is a good phrase. "Sally should have given me more encouragement" also works. With these comments, the self is safe and left to fail another day.

MARRIAGE BREAKDOWN

Minifights turn into larger fights, and larger fights turn into private wars. Separation and divorce seem to be a better alternative than compromise. The breakdown of the family unit becomes more critical each year. Sometimes, of course, it is the only solution, but many times it is only the easiest solution. Hindsight has demonstrated to many people that they've divorced too quickly. New problems usually replace the old ones, because in a divorce, you're forced to take at least half the problems with you.

We must admit that the independent nature of today's women has contributed to the increase in divorces. There are myriad reasons for divorce, but we can't deny the fact that there's a correlation. Many women have saved their lives because they've had an alternative to remaining in a dangerous marriage, but other women have decided they'd rather concentrate totally on themselves than share any of their time and attention with others. Separation and divorce bring their own brand of disappointment, failure, loneliness, and disillusionment. They also bring separation from children and/or the added responsibilities of children. Frequently divorce includes dealing with additional family problems when you eventually remarry and when your ex-spouse remarries. These new events all add up to more complications and frustrations on top of an already-full life of work and home responsibilities.

Many career-oriented people have recently decided that living together is the easy alternative to marriage. "All the benefits with none of the dangers or the responsibilities" seems to be the convincing phrase. Numerous working women believe this is the answer. The arrangement is somewhat removed from the traditional role of marriage yet brings all the comforts of home. A fortunate few may make this work, but again, it appears that more women find an unhappy conclusion. The frequent difficulty is still the division-of-labor problem that is common to marriage. Even if this is adequately worked out, another problem often develops, having to do with children.

Many (not all) career women find they want children as they get older. The absolute decisions of their twenties fade a little in the thirties. Somewhere between the ages of 30 and 37, a lot of them wonder what they've missed. They're no longer so confident they've made the best decision. Many times these women change 180 degrees, finding they want children more than anything else in their lives. The only problem is, where do they find the daddy?

Most live-in men aren't ready for this switch. They frequently have teenage or grown children from a previous marriage and aren't interested in starting again. Getting more than a little annoyed at the woman's attempt to change the game plan, they start feeling the walls closing in. This is only one way in which the supposedly easy alternative gets a little heavy. Perhaps Mary Miller, a 33-year-old single success story from New York, had the right idea when she answered Floyd's living-together suggestion like this: "I've already 'enjoyed' three intense relationships; let's try something a little less complicated—like marriage!"

STANDING ALONE—TOGETHER

Like anything worthwhile, marriage isn't easy. It's even more difficult when you have two strong personalities trying to make a go of it. Strong personalities usually like control and constantly jockey for the driver's seat. Although some homemakers also have strong personalities, there appears to be an even greater number of determined female personalities within the working ranks. We've learned to take care of ourselves in the outside world, and we're determined to take care of ourselves in the inside world as well. Given these facts, is it ever possible to live in harmony? Particularly, how

is it possible when there are all those extra demands that take time, energy, and attention away from the primary relationship? Is it possible to
stand alone, together?

I believe it is.

My husband and I talked about this issue a great deal before our marriage. He had been divorced, and I had been disillusioned concerning
marriage after observing the difficulties of many of my married friends. We
were also both pretty selfish, and we joked a little when we wrote our
marriage ceremony that we'd stay together "as long as we both shall dig it!"

We didn't actually include the "dig it" line, however. But I'm glad we
did include the following excerpt from Gibran's *The Prophet*. After a dozen
years together, it pretty well describes the way we live:

> You were born together, and together you shall be forevermore.
>   You shall be together when the white wings of death scatter your days.
>   Ay, you shall be together even in the silent memory of God.
>   But let there be spaces in your togetherness,
> And let the winds of the heavens dance between you.
>
> Love one another, but make not a bond of love:
>   Let it rather be a moving sea between the shores of your souls.
> Fill each other's cup but drink not from one cup.
>   Give one another of your bread but eat not from the same loaf.
> Sing and dance together and be joyous, but let each one of you be alone,
>   Even as the strings of a lute are alone though they quiver with the same
>   music.
>
> Give your hearts, but not into each other's keeping.
>   For only the hand of Life can contain your hearts.
> And stand together yet not too near together:
>   For the pillars of the temple stand apart,
> And the oak tree and the cypress grow not in each other's shadow. *

In daily living, this poetry doesn't work magically or easily. It begins
to make a real difference, however, with the realization that you can account only for yourself, even in something as intimate as marriage. The
acceptance of personal responsibility is crucial, because there are so many
things you *can* control once you actually begin doing it. Many times, this
personal control will affect your spouse, resulting in more support and
acceptance.

Each couple must look for and find the rhythm that works for them or
live with the consequences. These consequences can be a terrible mar-

* Kahlil Gibran, *The Prophet* (New York: Knopf, 1966), pp. 15–16.

riage, separation, or divorce. You only have to watch and evaluate a few marriages to find that what works for one couple won't necessarily work for another. Nevertheless, here are some ideas to try; they're outgrowths of the philosophy expressed in the poem above:

1. Don't attempt to own your spouse. You can't possess him anyway, so why try? Making unrealistic or unacceptable demands upon him doesn't add to your marriage; it usually helps to destroy it. What it does for certain is make *you* a demanding person, who usually has little to show for her efforts.

2. If he makes unrealistic demands on you, accept *some* of them (if the marriage is worth anything to you), but more importantly, *be certain you are growing beyond being degraded by his demands.* Many men will have some demanding ways; it's residue from the idea of a traditional marriage. It's hard for a man to get rid of all the traditional expectations even if he's trying. *But,* if you grow beyond these demands, they soon appear small and insignificant. You can incorporate them into the rhythm of your marriage—and live with them. Only you can determine when unrealistic demands move into the realm of unacceptable demands. Your alternatives to unacceptable demands are more serious, so you judge carefully when you decide which are unrealistic and which are unacceptable.

3. Enjoy activities alone. Don't be afraid to let him out of your sight; conversely, don't be afraid to get involved in activities without him. For goodness' sake, don't turn down a dinner invitation because he can't come! Enjoy specific activities together but also enjoy some alone. Also, find your own private place in the house, where you can be alone. See your alone time as a factor that will enable you to bring something new to your relationship, for what adds to you will likely add to him as well.

4. Make him happy. It will be a challenge on some days, but it's an activity that's preferable to focusing on all your problems. Very few people can stand apart from themselves long enough to feel the hurts of others. As his mate, you are the most likely person to try to help him lift his load. The strange beauty of helping someone else find happiness is that the act has the capacity of giving happiness back to us. The best payback is not the obligatory gift on Valentine's Day but rather the success of your efforts.

Most of these suggestions work best when the game is played two ways, but, as we said, you can control only yourself. "Yourself" is a big job. Some women might think some of these ideas suggest that a woman be used by a man, putting her back 75 years into another age. I don't agree, because I believe being used is a state of mind. You are used when you feel you are being used. Some women will scream for their women's lib manual if their husband asks for a pencil (and says "please"). Others can readily iron his shirts, cook his meals, and pick up his messes without feeling or being used. I believe it all has to do with the confidence you feel in yourself.

When you have a lot going on inside, your actions are very small in comparison. In the days when a woman's virginity was her big trump card, she was ruined if she lost it. In situations where a woman's biggest service to a man is the physical labor she performs around the house (and where she defines physical labor as degrading), she is degraded if she does physical labor. But, if a woman has more to offer to the relationship—if she has joy, a positive attitude, a developed mind, and a confident outlook—nothing can permanently cut her down. If she has it together, no one can take it away. Certainly, you're entitled to feeling "down" sometimes; that's what makes "ups" possible. But learn to fortify yourself so you become the source of strength, both for yourself and for those important to you.

THE TWO-CAREER MARRIAGE CAN BE THE BEST!

For all the difficulties we encounter from challenging the traditional balance in marriage, there are some benefits and *possible* advantages to a two-career marriage. I stress the word *possible* because these advantages are not always apparent. They can be developed, however, and with a sincere effort on the part of the marriage partners, these advantages will grow.

First of all, in a two-career marriage, there is a greater likelihood that both partners will be familiar with conflict resolution. When we have greater exposure to more people, more events, more miscommunications, and more failure, we become accustomed to handling conflict. Experience with managing conflict can put the differences we encounter within the marriage into a more realistic perspective. We can look at a situation more objectively, realizing that conflict is a natural part of human interaction.

On a monetary level, more money is a possible advantage to a two-career marriage. No one is saying that money buys happiness, but as the ancient Chinese philosopher said, money makes being miserable a lot more fun. More fights in marriage are over the issue of money (particularly the lack of it) than over any other issue. Having enough money to be comfortable helps the cause of marital bliss at least where finances are concerned.

Greater empathy is also possible when both partners in a marriage are working. The woman who works has a better understanding of the "jungle out there" than the woman who is isolated at home all day. Hopefully, the husband is also sharing the workload around the house, giving him greater insight into the pressures involved in managing a home. (We're still working on this, of course.) Additional empathy of any sort, however, is always beneficial to a marriage.

With two capable, responsible partners in a marriage, there is the chance that a marriage can develop to a higher level than the institution has ever before experienced. Marriage can move beyond the point of a support/dependency relationship (as in traditional marriage) through a period of overindependence (which leads to separation and divorce) to the better way: interdependency (two independent people choosing to depend on each other). In many ways, the idea of interdependency in marriage is still a dream. So far, there are very few models to follow—but there are some. I believe it's safe to hope there will be more in the future.

Finally, there's a better chance that the marriage partners in a two-career marriage can relate to the person they married instead of to the role they married. In a two-career marriage, each person becomes more individual, but at the same time, that individual has more to bring to the partnership. She becomes more than "the wife." He becomes more than "my old man." We get to a relationship between John Miller and Mary Jones Miller. With the separateness comes objectivity, and with objectivity comes less pressure. We are freer to live with, evaluate, and love our chosen partner.

INGREDIENTS FOR A HAPPY TWO-CAREER MARRIAGE

If someone could develop a panacea for marital misery, he or she could bottle it up and make a fortune. How nice it would be if it were that easy. But of course, it's not simple. As long as we have the ability to think, egos to develop, feelings to hurt, and wills to choose right or wrong, we are stuck with a certain amount of discord.

But with these same human qualities, we can work toward something better. We can make judgments, determine what is a better way for us, and decide to live in that way. Below is a list of 7 ingredients that are necessary for a happy two-career marriage. There are actually 14 thoughts, but I've paired them. Each thought seems to have a richer meaning when considered with a related thought. This can be true of human relationships as well. Here goes:

1. *Communication and Caring.* There are so many ways to communicate; verbal communication is only one way, although an important one. A look, a touch, a smile, a gleam in the eye, a glance—all are forms of communication that lay the groundwork for the verbal variety. I've coupled this thought with caring, for these communications should express caring. Even arguments should be handled within this framework. Of course, it's

difficult when you're angry, but it's the only way anyone wins a battle in marriage; and when one wins while caring, both win.

2. *Patience and Understanding.* The less time we have, the more patience we need. It's almost ironic: The rougher things get, the more we have to give.

When we're both working and conducting a marriage as well, we're burning the candle at both ends. We don't have as much time to clearly think through all situations, evaluate them carefully, and then act logically. Thus, misunderstandings develop. We thought we heard something that wasn't said; something was implied in a tone of voice we didn't appreciate; and we thought we overheard an under-the-breath comment that wasn't altogether complimentary. Misunderstandings all, and misunderstandings that require constant patience.

Physical exhaustion compounds the problem. Being physically worn out makes everything more difficult. How do we cope?

We develop patience. We learn to count to ten while waiting a little too long for loved ones; we learn to wait for an explanation one more time; and we learn to evaluate their negative comments in the light of their bad day. Patience and understanding: They must work together in a household that's busy and wants to be happy as well.

3. *Trust and Respect.* Part of the reason (perhaps the *whole* reason) many people are so possessive of their spouses is that they're afraid they'll betray them. This was a touchy issue when only one spouse worked outside the home, constantly faced with situations that presented temptations to stray from home. Of course, the at-home partner (usually the woman) had long suffered from attacks of jealousy and fear. Sometimes there was cause for her feelings of jealousy, and sometimes there was not.

With both partners in a marriage working outside the home, there is more than double the problem. Fears and jealousies feed on each other and help all sorts of negative feelings grow. Each spouse loses confidence and respect in the other; the longer this goes on, the more impossible the situation becomes.

Respect is the foundation for trust. When you treat your mate with respect and expect the best of him it is easy to trust him. Again, you cannot totally control his actions; you can only expect him to act in a responsible manner. He has no more control over you. When we expect the best, we frequently get the best.

When someone betrays that trust, he or she has not made a fool of the other party but has merely proved himself or herself to be untrustworthy. It takes a good deal of strength to feel this way, but truly, the betrayer has done the most harm to himself or herself—and additional harm to the relationship—but no harm directly to the innocent party. It is really incorrect to describe someone as the wronged party; the person who did the wrong is the loser. The innocent party still is all he or she was before, although a sadder person for an unhappy experience.

Concentrate on being trustworthy yourself. If you do, you are doing as much as you can. Expect your husband to behave in the same responsible manner.

4. *Excitement and Flexibility.* Habit has a strong hold on most of us. Habit dictates our actions, minute by minute, day by day. The older we get, the more difficult it is to break out of any particular habit. Habit is what we mean when we say someone gets set in her ways. Most people could happily conduct their lives by moving right along in the same groove. They don't live different years of their lives; they merely live the same year—over and over again.

People who enjoy this comfortable routine have only one major problem: change. What happens to them when something or someone goes against their neatly laid plan or settled way of life? In many cases, they are totally disoriented, unable to cope with the drastic change they are forced to accept.

Flexibility is a crucial ingredient in living, but it is particularly important when you are sharing your life with another person or other people. The more people who are intimate in your life, the more likely there will be unexpected events. The person who is flexible, the one who can roll with the punches, has the advantage over all others. The flexible person has greater peace of mind, for nothing can really happen that will throw her.

A step beyond flexibility is excitement. A person who wants excitement in her life can plan an African safari or climb the Himalayas, if she feels like it, but she can also find excitement in her own back yard. The world is full of new directions and adventure. No one could explore all the possibilities in her own hometown. In fact, no one could explore all the possibilities within herself or within the relationship with her spouse.

Flexibility in a person and within a relationship means a person can bend and move with the tide. Hopefully, one person will be ready and willing to bend a little farther than his or her partner at a time when the other person is being a little less flexible. And the thirst for excitement and new experiences enriches both individual and joint experiences in life. Fortunate, indeed, is the partner of a flexible, excitement-oriented person. Life is full of growth—for all involved.

5. *Sex and Intimacy.* Sex is overrated, overstated, overexposed, and overindulged. The focus on sex in our society has nearly stripped us all of any meaning in one of the finer gifts and experiences of life. Perhaps this overkill stems from our inability to define the higher-quality relationships and experiences. We can point to sex and be somewhat precise. We can count (and record, if we want to) the exact number of times we have

sexual intercourse, the exact number of people with whom we share sex, and we can even rate the quality of the orgasm, the variety of positions, the amount of foreplay, and so on. We are frequently left with negative feelings about our own experiences, which seem less in comparison with what everyone else is enjoying (or so we think). The sexual focus in our society has even managed to enter the marriage bed, making a monogamous relationship appear dull and limited.

Intimacy, on the other hand, is a related human need, but it involves so much more than the sex act. Intimacy involves the longing to be with another human being, the desire to share and to be part of a greater whole. Intimacy frequently involves sex, but intercourse alone can look pale by comparison. Warmth and intimacy can pay off, even at times when sex cannot.

Working couples need to give special consideration to the issues of sex and intimacy. Both experiences take time and energy to cultivate, and as we know, time and energy are in short supply in busy households. We are frequently too tired for much intimacy, and intimacy is the comfortable foundation and prelude for good sex. Couples—busy couples who want to be happy couples—would be smart to remember how easily they can sidestep this crucial element in marriage. Forget the ideas of your youth that sex must be spontaneous; there's little room for spontaneity in tight schedules, and time together happens only when it's planned. Plan to be alone together, and let nature take its course.

6. *Humor and Empathy.* Empathy gives us the capacity to truly feel and understand the needs and hurts of others; humor is the blessing that allows us to lighten the burdens of the pain we see, both in ourselves and in others. Without empathy, humor becomes harsh and cutting; it turns into a cold joke. On the other hand, empathy without humor renders us useless. We can cry with our spouse or friend, but we are little help.

Humor and empathy add the color to any relationship. Humor adds the subtle hues, making even the most painful experience a little more pastel. Empathy is the warm experience; it gives companionship and solace to the more difficult times we all experience. Empathy and humor balance each other, raising any relationship to something better.

7. *Toughness and Commitment.* No matter how much we work at marriage, the various attacks from the outside world can sometimes get to us. A hard day at the office can be the genesis of a big fight at home. A breakfast table turned battlefield can make anyone at the office appear to be a better alternative to what you have sharing your space and closets. Sometimes, no matter what you do to keep your marriage alive and interesting, the forces get to be too much. The "primary relationship" doesn't seem to be worth it.

Here's where you need toughness and commitment. You need, in fact, to be doubly tough and doubly committed. A good marriage, at times, is reduced to being nothing more than a commitment you've made. You realize that feelings and emotions are fickle and that there is something more permanent than whim. Pure commitment is the only attribute that can keep you stable when you feel the need to run. Since we know we are constantly changing, there are bound to be both high and low periods in any relationship. The peace in this realization, of course, is that whenever we're in low periods, we know it can get better. Conversely, when we're in high periods, we know we should treasure and enjoy the relationship, because it will soon be tested again.

Hundreds of women wrote and called me about the issues in this book, but one simple statement had a special message for all of us who are married. It was penned by a 51-year-old mother of four. Anna writes: "Most things involved [in my marriage] are just not serious enough to be considered problems. If it's important, it's talked out. After 32 years of marriage, my husband and I have a rapport that surpasses difficulties."

This is a worthy goal for any of us. Anna didn't say she had no difficulties; with a live-in mother-in-law and four children plus a husband and herself, there have probably been many difficulties in 32 years. Instead, she claims to have a "rapport that surpasses" the difficulties. This kind of rapport is developed through years of practice and concerns all the issues discussed above.

You may have noticed that Anna didn't claim it was love that surpassed the difficulties. You may also have noticed that I haven't included the word *love* anywhere in this discussion of the ingredients for a strong two-career marriage.

Love is not a sole ingredient for a sound marriage; it is all the characteristics listed above rolled into one. *Love* is also a problematic word, for it is used so flippantly in movies and literature. People are constantly falling in love, and falling out of love. Love isn't a ravine. Contrary to the impressions we glean from the movies, love isn't "never having to say you're sorry"; and it isn't "a special way of feeling," as expressed in a sentimental little book a few years back.

Most of us would do well to consider this definition of love from the Bible (I Corinthians 13:1–7 and 13). It provides some valuable insights for people of any religion or attitude:

> If I speak in the tongues of men and of angels, but have not love, I am a noisy gong or a clanging cymbal. And if I have prophetic powers, and understand all mysteries and all knowledge, and if I have all faith, so as to remove mountains, but have not love, I am nothing. If I give away all I have, and if I deliver my body to be burned, but have not love, I gain nothing.

Love is patient and kind; love is not jealous or boastful. It is not arrogant or rude. Love does not insist on its own way; it is not irritable or resentful. It does not rejoice at wrong, but rejoices in the right. Love bears all things, believes all things, hopes all things, endures all things. . . .
. . . There remain then, faith, hope, love, these three; but the greatest of these is love.

This passage on love removes love from the level of a flimsy feeling. It defines what love is and what love involves. It is far more—and far more demanding—than an emotional reaction. On the other hand, it leads to a far greater level of emotional intimacy than most people dare to imagine.

These words also point to the importance of sharing our lives with another, a very special other person. No matter what successes we have in life, without love, we are like a "noisy gong or a clanging cymbal." We only have to look around us to sense the wisdom of this statement. If we are lucky and mature in our approach to our marriage, we will love our spouse, in the fullest sense of the word. This love will give meaning to any other successes we may achieve. Some people will never have the chance at a good marriage and shouldn't feel they are a failure in life because of this, but the perspective and love of another can enhance any experience in life. This relationship should be treated with respect and given all the time and attention it deserves.

PLANNING AS A TEAM

Most of us want our marriages to survive, despite the many challenges we encounter in this hectic, demanding world. As the statistics show, it's getting more and more difficult each year to stay together. Marriage is actually a very fragile institution, and so a couple truly interested in maintaining marital harmony should take some positive steps to see that they're putting the odds in their favor. One of the best ways to do this is to plan for the future, together.

Back in Chapter 3, we discussed the importance of goals and priorities. Goals and priorities are the basis for planning as a team as well as the basis for planning as an individual.

It goes without saying that to plan as a team, both partners on the team should agree that planning is worthwhile. It's pretty hard to plan as a team if only one member is willing. Some husbands who are already quite aware of the power and importance of planning for success will be anxious to plan your life together more carefully. Other husbands will be surprised and happy to discover you're interested in doing this activity together, particularly if they had been feeling that your career is more important than your marriage (as many husbands of working women seem to feel). Then again, convincing your husband to plan with you might require your special persuasive technique. Anything's fair for this good cause. Planning together is bound to be an interesting exercise, while also being extremely worthwhile.

Begin planning together by working separately. Agree that you will each evaluate your individual strengths, your individual personal preferences and enjoyments in life, and your individual long-term goals on paper. Long-term goals are defined as goals you set for yourself at least three years down the road. Let your thoughts mellow a little and agree to meet to talk about this subject a few days later. Personally, I believe it's better to give this a week. It's frequently the first time most people have put any real thought into this.

When you get together to discuss your ideas, make certain you're both as relaxed as possible and have some quiet time together. Both husband and wife can find this an extremely interesting encounter, for they frequently find out things about their spouse they never knew before this exercise. It can be a real eye-opener!

Once you've shared your thoughts, compare your lists. Look for complementary strengths, mutual interests, and common long-term goals. Hopefully, there will often be a number of similarities. Talk about what these similarities can and should mean to you. Are you currently doing all you can to enhance these aspects of your marriage?

Time, again, for separate thinking. During this period, each person should try to set priorities on long-term goals for the two of you and your family. If you found you had more needs and desires than you had time, priorities are absolutely necessary.

Again, share your thoughts with your mate during some good, quiet time together. Decide which goals are best for you as a family. See how each of you can use your strengths and skills to move your family unit toward those goals. Begin identifying short-term goals that will eventually lead to your long-term goals. Concentrate on the activities you each can do within the next month or two that will move you in the right direction.

What will be the possible obstacles? Who or what outside of the two of you would help you as a couple to achieve your goals? Discuss these important questions and look for the best answers. There will be obstacles, of course, so planning for them is the best way to overcome them.

Make a definite commitment to each other. It's best to put these commitments in writing. Indicate your plan carefully; identify the role of each person involved; set target dates for completion.

Of course, some of these goals may be more important to one person than to the other, but as a team, both members can contribute to some of the goals. Dreams may be very individual, but when planning as a team, you've had time to evaluate the personal dreams against the dreams of the unit; you've been able to evaluate the price of a personal goal that may be an obstacle to achieving the goal you set together. Some of these personal goals can be successfully realized anyway, if both partners search for ways to maximize the satisfaction and happiness of all parties.

Planning and cooperation are the keys—and they work better than just playing it all by ear, letting things fall where they may, taking a shot at it and seeing what happens, and so on. Your life together is far too important. Use the skill of planning, which you know is important in your professional life, to enhance, enrich, and support your personal life. The technique is the same, and the result is quite frequently success!

TURNING THE EGO INTO "US"

We must truly work at "making" love in marriage, because there is a great deal of evidence that loving doesn't come naturally. We are all very selfish by nature, concentrating on our needs and wants alone. To reap all the benefits marriage has for us, however, we are called on to rise above our primal instincts in order to become something more. We are required to give to another person an important part of ourselves. This point is made clearly when we recall that "Lust seeks to get; love seeks to give."

Perhaps logic gets in our way. It seems logical that if we give something to another person, we must necessarily have less left for ourselves. This is true of monetary, tangible things, but it is not true of human emotions and feelings. We can gain only by giving away in the areas that are ultimately important to us.

By the time we've grown and seen the world with its problems, disappointments, and hardships, we begin to realize that love is more than a sentimental emotion. As we strive and succeed in the business world, let's not lose the important things we already have in our lives. When we close the door to our offices at 5:00 P.M., let's make certain we can head home to something worthwhile. If that "something" is a good marriage, we have the best of both worlds.

8

THE CHILDREN

OR

There's treachery beneath those bright, shining faces

KIDS? NO THANK YOU

Having children is one of the most intense experiences life has to offer. Children add to life in every sense: They add joy, pleasure, and an identification with the future. But they also add pain, despair, and a host of problems that must be solved immediately! Many people feel that children are central to a woman's nature, while others will argue that having children is a big part of the trap that has kept women in a secondary role in society.

Arguments get hot and heavy when it comes to the subject of children. One side of the argument maintains that children are life itself— that they are the future of mankind and that we do our duty as living beings when we "pay back" life with new life. Never mind about personal sacrifice; the cost is not the issue. The decision to have children should not be based purely on one's own comfort and desire for emotional rewards. One has children for life and for the future, not for oneself.

The other side of the argument advances the idea that it's all right to think of yourself first, that you owe nothing to the ambiguous future. People who decide against children give many rational reasons for their decision: "The future is too uncertain," "I'm so busy, it wouldn't be fair to the children," "We really can't afford it," "I don't want to be tied down," and "I'm afraid I wouldn't be a good parent." From a rational point of view, most of these arguments make a lot of sense. The majority of people who approach parenthood in this "rational" way usually decide not to indulge, thank you.

Fourteen years ago, when my husband and I were still in the dating stage, we frequently enjoyed our visits with Carol and Phil, a couple who were approaching the big Four-Oh (40). Phil had been raised in a family of nine kids and had watched his siblings carefully as they went through the ups and downs of child rearing. Carol, raised in a family of three, was always busy, but was also concerned about time running out for her if she ever wanted to be a mother. They had been married for over ten years, and it was time to decide.

One evening before dinner at their home, they sat down on their living room couch; their two pairs of eyes stared at us intently. Phil had two sheets of paper in his hand as he explained to us: "We're trying to decide whether or not to have children. We've been making our pro and con list; it seems the con side is winning. What do you think?"

My mind went absolutely blank. I really hadn't thought of children at all. My future husband had children, and we played with them now and then in the summer but then returned them to their mother in the fall. Besides, we hadn't talked of marriage as yet, much less children. We listened politely as they aired their thoughts to us. They eventually decided not to have kids and continue to lead overbusy lives to this day. I honestly don't know if they've ever had second thoughts about their decision, but I can remember Phil saying, "There's no guarantee they'll grow up to like you anyway!" They're probably very happy with their decision.

During my research for this book, a number of working women wrote me about their decision not to have children. Janice Wagner, a 35-year-old self-employed operator of a public relations agency, has been married 11 years and has no children. She wrote of her decision, shared with her husband, not to get involved in parenting:

> I guess there's a bit of defensiveness [in not having children], not because we have any significant doubts about our choice, but because others do not accept our decision very well.
>
> I come from a large, Catholic family—and all my cousins on both sides have lots of kids. For the first few years of our marriage, it was assumed that we would begin having children right away. We've been married for almost 12 years now, and the family has begun to accept the fact that we will not have children—at least they are not voicing their feelings out loud to us.
>
> I'm not really sure where and when we decided not to have children. I've done some soul-searching to try to figure out my feelings about children. When I look back on my own childhood, it was pretty happy. But

even as a youngster, when other girls were playing with their baby dolls dreaming about the day when they would have their own babies, I was playing with grown-up dolls and dreaming about the day I would be able to wear high heels and go to work in a very important job. In fact, I never did imagine children in my future.

Before Jim and I married, we discussed children, and Jim's feelings were pretty much the same as mine. After eight years of marriage—and a lot of discussion—Jim had a vasectomy. I can't say we never had doubts that we made the right decision. I guess in any important decision there are always doubts. I had one brief flash of doubt right after Jim had his vasectomy—but I think I was lamenting the fact that the decision was irreversible, not that the decision was wrong.

We both like children—and we have lots of friends with children who will "lend" them to us for a few days or even a week at a time. In many ways, we are children ourselves—I don't think adults really grow up until they have children and have to become grown up.

AN "ABOUT-FACE"

I well understand the feelings expressed by Janice. I had many of the same thoughts and concerns during the first six years of my marriage. But I also had stepchildren to complicate the issue. After our marriage, the children seemed to spend more time with us than I had anticipated. (I've found this frequently happens. Many a career woman married to a divorced man finds that his kids don't stay with their mother, according to the original plan. The visits get longer and longer.) I was fortunate in that I truly loved my stepchildren and got along with them well. Our relationship was made somewhat easier because I married their father when they were still pre-schoolers, and they grew with me. Also, my husband let me deal with his children the way I saw fit; he didn't continually try to step in while I was developing a relationship with the kids. His ex-wife was also instrumental in keeping everything on an even keel; she talked well of us to the children, and we returned the courtesy. It all worked smoothly, it seemed to me. I had two beautiful children for three months during the summer (while their mother had a break), and then we returned them to her, regaining all the freedom of a childless couple. I read books that advocated the childless life and even celebrated a nonmother version of Mother's Day. I knew I had the best of all worlds—two lovely kids, but very few responsibilities.

But then, shortly after my thirtieth birthday, my father died. As I suggested in Chapter 1, he was very dear to me, and his death affected me profoundly. As I was packing my suitcase to fly to his deathbed, I said to my husband, Merrill, "I've got to tell Dad I'm going to have a baby!" It was absolutely the first time I ever had such a thought.

During those traumatic weeks just before he died, I sat next to my father's bed and wiped his brow. We talked of many things, and children was one of them. He had six children; I was the oldest. We all always knew we were his whole life, and he loved all of us and our mother with his whole heart. I told him I wanted to have a baby. His weary face brightened considerably—"How wonderful that would be for you!" Within six months after his funeral, I was pregnant. When you promise your cherished father on his deathbed you're going to have a baby, there is no other choice!

Physically the pregnancy was easy, but emotionally it was very trying. My husband was as uncomfortable as I was about the change that was coming into our free-and-easy life. A few months before the baby was due, I set a bassinet in the middle of the living room. I thought it would give us a chance to get used to the idea. I watched as my husband circled to avoid the intrusion; I frequently did the same thing. We attended our Lamaze classes (a first for both of us) and watched my tummy bloom.

And then Jennifer was born. Merrill was present and totally involved in her birth; he tickled her tiny chin before the cord was cut. Both of us will remember that day always; our apprehension immediately flew out the window as our lives filled with joy. My entire perspective on children changed. I couldn't believe I used to be so violently against having one of my own! Today, five years later, she means more to us than ever. My stepchildren are now teenagers, and they and Jennifer are definitely brother and sisters. We love them all very much and can't imagine not having them.

Today, I try to be understanding and modern as I listen to other couples explain their choice not to have children. I nod my head politely as they state, "We don't have the time," "We don't want to be tied down," and so on. I remember well the time I shared their opinion and realize how sincerely they mean what they say!

But I can't help feeling a little sorry for them because they don't know better. They've all played the "What if?" games as they've watched their friends and siblings with their children. They've tried to imagine themselves in the same role. All of my friends and one of my brothers had children long before I did; even though they had very nice children, I was always glad the kids went home with them and not with me.

The "What if?" game is totally useless. There is absolutely no comparison between watching other people's children and having your own. If you are unable to have children for one reason or another, that's one story, but to consciously choose to miss the experience is indicative of very narrow sights. Of course, you'll live a comparatively hassle-free life, but you're also passing up one of life's richest gifts. A very few may be better off as nonmothers, but too many are making this decision who would simply *glory* in motherhood. Of course, there would be compromises and difficult decisions, but we all know that anything worthwile requires mind-boggling choices. The reward, however, is riches; it's life at its fullest, for children are, themselves, *life!*

I've thought carefully about taking this openly prochildren stand. The alternative, of course, was to write with noninvolvement, opting for the "it's up to each individual to make her choice" approach. It *is* up to each individual, of course, but I feel an obligation to share my 180-degree shift in attitude. Perhaps my experience will encourage other ambitious women with definite career goals to take a second look at their nonmotherhood decision. I'm certainly glad there was an event in my life—albeit a very sad one for me—that made me reconsider.

"THE URGE"

Sometimes it doesn't take a traumatic event for a woman to suddenly decide she wants a child. In November 1981 *McCall's* magazine published a controversial article entitled "Baby Hunger." In this article, author Lois Leiderman Davitz explores the urge to have a baby that many older non-mothers suddenly feel. Davitz describes her own experience in this way:

> When I was about 29, something strange happened. Even now, many years later, I vividly recall sensations of an inner awakening, a deeply emotional urge that seemed to increase daily. I suddenly became focused on babies in the supermarket and had my eye out for pregnant women. My newfound awareness of children and a growing desire that I didn't seem able to submerge led me to announce one morning to my stunned husband that I wanted a baby. Less than a year later, our first child was born. *

Davitz's article caused a furor among the female editors of childbearing age on *McCall's* staff. Most were furious that the psychologist was suggesting that having babies was somehow instinctive. Most of them maintained the "drive" was culturally conditioned. The article ended with an editor's note requesting readers to share their own experiences with "baby hunger."

Two months later, *McCall's* reported its mail had been heavy—and emotionally charged. Like many on the *McCall's* staff, some of the readers

* p. 10.

thought it absolutely silly that anyone would believe having babies was instinctive. About 90 *percent* of the mail, however, was sympathetic with Dr. Davitz's theory. Two of the responses *McCall's* published in January 1982 * were:

> As much as I would like to deny it, perhaps women *do* have the instinct to have babies (and whenever I have heard a man say that, I have generally gone for his throat!).

> I sometimes feel as if my body is betraying me—making me yearn for something that my mind tells me is impractical. I find myself thinking about babies and wondering what our children would be like.

Dr. Davitz has a strong point concerning the urge to have a baby. I have seen it many times, even in the most convinced "baby haters." Of course, it is emotionally charged, because having children is central to the entire controversy generated over the home/work conflict in women. Many women see children as the factor that keeps females from achieving all they might be able to achieve through equality with men. The following is one negative comment from the January 1982 article. This woman speaks well for many adamant nonmothers like herself:

> No wonder some people still see women as emotional, inferior beings. I cannot believe that any thinking person could regard [instinctual baby hunger] as even remotely credible. Just about all of my friends feel the way I do about children—we don't like them, pure and simple. †

Women such as the one quoted above will probably live a contented life without children. Of course, today they have the right and the technology to make this decision. They are also free from the compromises all working mothers are forced to make on a regular basis, for the decision to have a baby is only the beginning. Motherhood is truly the one irreversible decision of our lives, in addition to being one of the most difficult.

JUGGLING THE COMPROMISES

Many women who have established their careers before having children believe it will be easy to return to work six weeks after the baby is born. Some actually do this with few qualms or misgivings. Far more women,

* "That Urge to Have a Baby," *McCall's*, January 1982, pp. 8 and 10.
† Ibid., p. 113.

however, return to work with many doubts and conflicting feelings. In addition to loving their own baby far more than they imagined possible, they find it's more difficult to leave the baby than they had expected. Even those women who are lucky enough to find good child care are unsure they're making the right decision. Many women who even feel it's best for the child to be a little independent of mother feel sorry for themselves because they're missing so much of their child's development. Children are babies for such a short time; why should we give it up?

The answer for many women is that this is part of the sacrifice of being a working mother. If a woman chooses to stay home for a few years while her children are small, she loses her place on the corporate ladder—a place she may have fought long and hard to obtain. The decision-making process is agonizing; the final decision is never totally acceptable. If she chooses to stay home, she will likely be unhappy; if she chooses to con-tinue working, she will also run into days when she can hardly bear to leave her small child. It's the classic no-win situation.

Not only does the little one pull on your time; he or she also pulls on your dedication and energy. It is extremely difficult to be alive, interested, and perky for an 8:00 A.M. meeting after spending the night with a sick or crying child. You're tired, and your mind is at home. You have addi-tional problems if you left your infant crying at the sitter's as you headed off to work. No matter if your child is 20 miles away, you can hear that baby crying!

It doesn't get much easier as they grow older. Naturally, the older chil-dren have fewer sleepless nights, so that problem finally disappears, but you are still left with the compromises involved with their care and needs. Many women believe teenagers can take care of themselves. The consen-sus seems to be that the older they get, the more acceptable it is to work outside the home. This sounds good, but many women have found that raising teenagers is the most difficult of all. Teenagers don't believe they need mama, but they frequently do—even if it's only to talk. And many women maintain that your children never leave you; even when they're grown and supposedly on their own, they still frequently need their mother.

Guilt can be overwhelming. Louise Young, a 38-year-old working mother of three young girls, puts it this way:

At times, I am consumed with guilt, but to be honest, I know I'd be miserable as a full-time mother. My mother grew up believing her ultimate goal in life was to be a wife and mother. When she achieved it, she felt rewarded. I worked hard in school and learned to seek different kinds of achievement. I worked for and earned a career. I wouldn't be happy at home, and certainly my children would feel the results of having an unhappy, frustrated, and unfulfilled mother. Things have changed since my mother's generation. When I was a child, all the women and all the children on my block were home 90 percent of the time. Today, one woman on my block is a full-time mother, and 90 percent of the children are enrolled in nursery school, gymnastics classes, diaper dip, or some such. At home, there is no companionship for me from other mothers and no companionship for my children from other children. In many ways, they are better off at the Montessori school where they have been since age two. It's a tremendously stimulating environment full of all kinds of other children.

A couple of weeks ago I was feeling guilty because my eldest daughter, age seven, will probably never get to be a Girl Scout. Then I realized that she will go on business trips with my husband and me to Pennsylvania; Washington, D.C.; Deep Creek Lake, Maryland; and Walt Disney World this year, not to mention seeing behind the scenes at innumerable TV stations, the zoo, and other places we visit. I decided it balanced out. The older the children get, the more we can include them in things we do.

I'm raising children, girls, who will be even more goal-oriented than I am. They are thoroughly modern kids, very much a part of our business lives. We take them with us a lot when we have to work nights or weekends. They are living fast-paced, exciting lives by comparison to my childhood. Maybe it's not the idea I grew up with of how to raise children, but maybe I've been feeling guilty more than I should. One thing I know for sure: My children know they are loved. I may not be with them all day every day, but they know they are loved.

It helps me to realize that even stay-at-home mothers have periods of doubts, apprehensions, and uncertainties. Working women have a lifestyle that differs from the traditional model, so there is a tendency to blame their jobs for anything and everything that goes wrong. "If only I had stayed home, this wouldn't have happened!" is a frequent and easy chastisement. We are all so eager to accept the blame for the way things turn out. It's difficult to maintain the perspective that problems and misfortunes are part of living and find us all, even when there's no one to blame. If we didn't care so deeply for our children, it wouldn't bother us so deeply.

ATTITUDES TOWARD BEING A MOTHER

There are no rule books that tell us what makes a good mother and what makes a bad mother. The majority of us do the best we can and let the kids take it from there. Actually, that's all any of us can do. But since there's no rule book for motherhood, no one can tell us that the best mothers are those who stay at home and raise kids as a full-time occupation. Granted, full-time motherhood is the way it's been done by most women from the birth of the Industrial Revolution until approximately 1960, but that doesn't mean it's the best way. Again, attitudes should be developed based on the main goal: launching happy, healthy, productive human beings. When you think of the goal for what it is, instead of focusing on the means to reach this goal, many new possibilities become apparent. You don't necessarily raise "happy, healthy, productive human beings" by keeping a spotless house or being the busiest member of the P.T.A. Many traditional mothers have been misfocused on such activities. Consider Louise Young's letter above. She was feeling guilty for not having the time and inclination to enroll her oldest daughter in the Girl Scouts—until she took into account the many opportunities open to her daughter that she had missed in her own childhood. She also realized that her children *knew* they were loved. Love, along with encouragement and respect, are big aids when it comes to raising the kinds of children we all want.

There is also a dangerous tendency in many mothers—particularly many traditional mothers—to treat the members of their family, especially their children, as possessions. Not one woman in a thousand would ever admit to treating her family in this manner, but it is true, nevertheless. For such women, their family is their job, and they are the ruler of the roost, the mistress of the household. Many would probably make good leaders in the business world, if only they weren't committed to *running* the household. Consider the accompanying illustration, published sometime during the 1800s, and you get an idea of one artist's perception of motherhood at that time.

This possessive attitude is extremely harmful to developing human beings. It stifles children and makes them weak and dependent. Even though many of these women would be highly insulted at the accusation, many of them are *not* good mothers. They are selfish and demanding. They are also failing in their main task of launching responsible human beings.

In the last chapter, I quoted from Gibran's *The Prophet*. He is equally insightful "On Children":

> Your children are not your children.
>   They are the sons and daughters of Life's longing for itself.
> They come through you, but not from you.
>   And though they are with you yet they belong not to you.
>
> You may give them your love but not your thoughts,
>   For they have their own thoughts.

Source: Harold H. Hart, ed., *Humor, Wit, and Fantasy* (New York: Hart Publishing, 1976).

You may house their bodies but not their souls,
    For their souls dwell in the house of tomorrow, which you cannot visit,
        not even in your dreams.
You may strive to be like them, but seek not to make them like you.

For life goes not backward nor tarries with yesterday.
    You are the bows from which your children as living arrows are sent forth.
The archer sees the mark upon the path of the infinite, and He bends you
    with His might that His arrows may go swift and far.

Let your bending in the archer's hand be for gladness;
    For even as He loves the arrow that flies, so He loves also the bow
        that is stable. *

As working mothers, we are less likely to be as domineering toward our children. We have the opportunity to back off from them each day, allowing us a more objective view. As we work, we are also exposed to many other values and ways of living. Many of these lifestyles are not to our liking, but they do help us put those near and dear to us in perspective. We become a little more content to live and let live. We have a better chance to see our children as the individuals they are instead of as an extension of ourselves.

* Kahlil Gibran, *The Prophet* (New York: Knopf, 1966), pp. 17–18.

LAUNCHING WITH POSITIVES

Many people believe all it takes to raise decent kids is common sense. Certainly common sense is preferable to no sense at all, but common sense is not enough. Love is a very special ingredient, but it takes far more than love. It takes constant positive encouragement, continual positive strokes, and eyes that are blind to obvious stupidity.

Criticism is very easy and comes naturally. Many women have suffered silently as they received the brunt of their husband's pent-up frustrations. Of course, women at home experienced many frustrations as well, so there were always more than enough frustrations to go around that caused continual criticism and sparring at the dinner table and afterward.

With many women entering the job market, there are even more frustrations to bear. There are more demands and more chances for failure, aggravations, antagonisms. The children, more than ever, are likely to suffer unless we take special measures to treat them with particular concern. This treatment takes pure determination and constant effort.

Watch the criticism. Replace it with positive comments at all times. This is not a "spare the rod" approach; it is a common-sense approach that works! I was an adult before I realized this was the approach my parents used on me. In the two short years I taught school, I saw this work!

Robert was one of the most difficult 12 year olds ever to walk into a seventh-grade classroom. His reputation preceded him, for I had heard about him frequently in the teacher's lounge. He was the youngest of four brothers—and a real "pill."

Robert lived up to his reputation. Although many seventh graders approach "impossible," Robert was already there. He demanded *constant* attention and would do whatever he had to do to get it. He'd make strange noises with any part of his body that would respond; make faces at the other students; rustle papers; cause a commotion using rubber bands, desks, books—you name it.

One day, in total despair, I resorted to the school's child psychologist. She was convinced that behavior modification was the answer. "Sure!" I thought. "Here you sit in a quiet room off the library and tell me to ignore his negative behavior and praise his good behavior. There's only one problem—he's *always* bad and *never* good!" But I decided there was nothing else left to try. The next day was to be Robert's day—all the way. I had to deal with Robert if I was ever going to get anywhere with the rest of the class.

As soon as I began discussing the day's lesson, Robert began making his favorite noises. I ignored him and kept on talking to the other students. The noises got louder and louder, and still I said nothing to him. I kept my eyes focused on other students (who surprisingly kept their eyes on me!).

Getting nowhere, Robert decided to try a different tactic. He slithered out of his chair onto the floor. While still making noises, he moved like a snake across the back of the classroom. I kept on talking about the lesson of the day, although in my mind I was killing him.

He moved to the back of the room on my right, approaching the resource materials I had spent years accumulating while in college. Suddenly he found a pencil and got another idea. With obvious anger, he began stabbing at my materials, punching holes in all my boxes!

Pure stubbornness alone kept me from saying anything to him. I was determined!

A very few minutes later, he was in front of the room, standing his full 5'3". He walked slowly up to me and faced me squarely, his back to his classmates. I looked right through him and kept talking. He stared at me in amazement. Finally he waved his arms back and forth in front of me; I kept on talking and moved on to the next question. He was finally silent.

I felt my stomach tighten, however, as he headed to my left and to my desk. As he began jamming my stapler into the cement wall, I made my move: "Class, I want to thank you all for being so attentive to me during some trying circumstances. I appreciate your efforts very much. As a reward, you may all be dismissed early. I'd like you to quietly go outside and get some fresh air before your next class. Thanks again!"

Then I called their names and thanked them, one by one, as I dismissed them. I called on everyone in the classroom but Robert, who sat speechless at my desk. He was the only one left in the room as I followed the other students outdoors. I was exhausted.

The next day I was ready for Robert. As his class filed into my room, I caught him by the shoulder at the doorway. He looked sheepish and very little. "Robert, I need your help. Will you please try? I know you're really a good boy, we just have to figure out how good boys act! Let's help each other!"

He smiled and said he'd really try for me. A few minutes later he worked for five whole minutes on his lesson before he started acting up. He had agreed that when he just "couldn't" behave anymore, he'd help me out by behaving and working in the hall. Five minutes of work was better than he had ever done, so that was progress.

That afternoon I wrote a note to his parents. I explained to them that I realized they had continually heard of all the trouble Robert caused, so I thought they'd like to hear from the teachers when he behaved himself. I explained that he had worked hard for "nearly 15 minutes" that afternoon (I stretched the truth a bit!) and that I was very proud of him. Robert beamed as he read this most unusual note to his parents. I can't say Robert was totally trouble-free from that point on, but I can honestly report he continued to improve.

The point of this story is that a child responds to positive comments much better than to negative ones. If we continually tell him, "Robert, you're such an idiot! You never do anything right! You're an absolute fool! You'll never grow up to amount to anything!"—Robert will probably believe us. How can we expect him to grow up to be kind, intelligent, confident, and secure when we've spent years telling him he's just the opposite?

The fortunate point for working parents is that positive reinforcement takes very little time, once we develop the habit of giving it. You can praise for such little things, and the good words mean so much, particularly from someone who's important. Kids of all ages will benefit if you start today. (Husbands also appreciate and respond to positive comments!) If you must, write "Ps" on your schedule, reminding yourself to give your loved ones the "positives." It may be one of the most important things you do all day! Positive reinforcement will not guarantee that your children will grow up problem-free, but this type of communication will insure that you've laid the important groundwork for handling problems. All parents, both working and nonworking, need all the help they can get. And since working parents must make every minute count, don't forget to administer daily doses of positive strokes. Certainly you're entitled to point out mistakes once in a while, but be certain they're important—and outweighed by positive comments at least ten to one!

WHAT A MOTHER IS NOT

A mother is not a servant. This point should be made perfectly clear to children from the day they are born. Fortunate children have parents who make this point even if they have mothers who are full-time homemakers. Children with working mothers are lucky, because they must learn this well if they expect to have any time with their mothers at all—and to have a mother who's worth being with!

If you begin early training your children to realize that you are not their servant, you'll have an easy task. If the kids have never been waited upon, they won't expect it. On the other hand, changes are still possible, even with older children. Some women have done it:

> We talked a great deal about ERA and women's rights. My sons, who were about 13 and 15, sure could agree—except where chores were involved.

They had always had some responsibilities but were now being asked to do more. We talked about how being born female did not mean I liked housework, washing, cooking, etc.; I liked it a lot less when the rest of the family had free time on weekends and I was playing "catch up." We also talked about what my career meant to me and what my paycheck meant to the family—educational benefits, vacations, etc. Well, it sure isn't perfect, but we've come a long way! (One added benefit of all this is knowing my sons have developed an awareness and understanding of the women's rights issues. I feel it is the responsibility of those of us who are the mothers of sons to develop and nurture this attitude.)

On the weekends, we all work together. With five people in one house, we have to help each other. The boys can cook a simple meal, wash the clothes, dust and vacuum, and take care of the yardwork. I just keep telling them that housework is not a one-person job. If there are five people under one roof, then there are five people who have to keep that roof in running condition. It's not fair to burden one person with all the work. We also are a family-oriented group and like to do things together, so working is just part of family life.

These women are ladies after my own heart! I have long professed that "the mother in this house does not like doing all the work, contrary as this might be to your impression of mothers in general." For the sake of all family members—a mother is not a servant.

Nor is a mother capable of living her children's lives. This need in some women goes back to the tendency to dominate the entire family. Part of the desire to run her children's lives, however, comes from the natural wish of a mother not to see her children hurt. We know so many of the pitfalls ourselves—because we fell in—and we don't want our children to make the same mistakes. We want to save them from all hurts—emotional, physical, and spiritual. We want them to become more than we have been able to be. We push them toward our dreams.

But as Gibran said, this is wrong. Our children have their own dreams. They live in a different time. They have unique needs and skills. As parents, we can guide, direct, and encourage. We can also get to suffer with them as they make their own mistakes. The only advice we can ever really give is the advice that is requested. Living our own lives is job enough. Fortunately, if we live them with honesty, courage, and style, we are doing the most for our children that we possibly can: We are setting a good example. By working outside the home and managing the home as well, we are showing our children how this difficult juggling act is done. Our sons and daughters should have an easier task; if they do, we should be proud of ourselves!

Another thing to keep in mind: A stepmother is not a mother. With over 50 percent of all marriages ending in divorce, that strange person called a "stepparent" is becoming more and more common. Unfortunately, since the days of Snow White and Cinderella, a stepmother has had a bad reputation. Many of us know this reputation is undeserved, and we're stuck with the task of improving it.

There is no question that the issue of mixed families adds extra pressures to family life, and mixed families are extremely common to working women. There are some important insights I've gained after many years as a stepmother, a mother, and now a stepdaughter as well. (Of course, I believe the insights are valid for stepfathers, too.) I'd like to share them:

1. You are not the child's real mother. We each get but one "real" mother. Those of us who pretend to be the real one are making a mistake and are opening ourselves to unnecessary heartaches.

You cannot force warm feelings upon anyone; each person, no matter how young, is in charge of his or her own feelings. All my stepchildren have reacted to me differently, and I have developed different relationships with each of them over the years. I'm very happy with them and feel fortunate they have been the bonuses of my marriage. Of course, they have added problems and concerns to my life that I wouldn't have had without them, but my philosophy of children holds that they *are* life; thus, *all* their ups and downs are worthwhile and part of the game.

2. Their father is not your personal possession. Any husband is a mate, not a possession; but a father owes time and allegiance to others besides his wife. It's easier for most women to share a man with children they have produced together, but if she marries a man who already has children, she must share him with them. Sometimes this includes his sharing some of his time and attention with the children's mother, particularly when it involves issues concerning the children. This is part of the reality of subsequent marriages.

3. Don't try to compare yourself to the children's natural mother. If you do, you're playing a no-win game. Children will play any and all advantages to get what they want. They will play their father against their mother when the two are married to each other (I did it!) and will push even further when their parents are divorced. Pitting mother against stepmother is a natural—and generally effective—move. Facing off a stepmother against a father is also a good ploy. Anything for their own personal wants and desires. Some are trickier at this than others; some manage to look innocent through it all. Some are very subtle but keep working away at it. The poor parents never know what hit them. The kids play on any and all insecurities and needs.

The smart parents are ready for this. They tell the kids to "sit on it," and they don't let them gain an inch. Whenever possible, they compare notes with other parents to get the real picture. This eventually turns out better for all concerned. Once the kids realize you're ready for them, they back off and act comparatively decent. It's just that at first there's an irresistible temptation for them to say, "You're not a good mommy; my *real* mommy is better than you!"

4. Speaking of your predecessor(s)—don't. Don't, unless you have something good to say, that is. Nothing is gained when you present negative comments, and the children can be very seriously hurt. The children should be given an opportunity to make their own judgments, as they eventually will despite your efforts. If you have presented a negative picture of their absent parent, you will be the one whom they'll judge negatively in the long run. You're never wrong if you emphasize the good qualities in all members of the families involved. You present a positive example yourself by doing so.

5. A stepparent (possibly) provides a unique kind of assistance to child rearing. Numerically, three or four heads can be better than one or two, but there's also a different dimension that the natural parent seldom has. That dimension is objectivity.

Most of us get too intense with our own children. We demand so much of them, having too much of ourselves wrapped up in them. We are also totally responsible for them. This can be a heavy burden and very taxing. The burden makes it extremely difficult to make helpful judgments, because our vision is so clouded by emotions.

A stepmother can be a special help from where she stands. She can love the child and be concerned for his or her welfare, but the drive, the absolute insistence, the intensity, are easier to avoid. This provides the child with a loving adult who can also be a friend. It's a very special feeling for all involved. The perspective can also add some insights to your attitude toward your natural-born children.

6. A stepmother must learn, even more than a parent, to be flexible. She must be ready to love and organize 2 to 20—whoever's in residence at a particular time. We have a very mobile society, and children can come and go. It's much easier if you can roll with the punches, setting up everything from bunk beds to a new housecleaning schedule at a minute's notice. Most of all, you have to hang loose. Just when you believe everyone is happily settled, a 15 year old can announce she's going to live with another parent—and she disappears. A generally tranquil exterior is no indication of inner calm or inner turmoil. The same uncertainty develops in children who live with both natural parents; it's just that stepchildren

have alternatives that nonstep families lack. Learn to smile, and go with what you have.

GETTING THE KIDS TO HELP

Many of us would agree with Ogden Nash: "Parents were invented to make children happy by giving them something to ignore." This comment seems particularly pertinent to the subject of helping around the house. Children have a natural talent for making messes but generally lack the natural tendency to pick things up! They're busy "growing" and can't be bothered with mundane things such as cleaning rooms, doing dishes, washing clothes, and so forth. That is, they can't be bothered unless they have a strong, together mother who teaches them responsibility. It takes energy and determination to accomplish this feat, but many women have shown *it can be done.*

Infants and preschoolers usually think housework is fun (what do they know?), so use this misperception to your advantage. A two year old can sort clothes, pick up toys, fold washcloths, and haul the empty garbage bins back up the driveway. A four year old can make a bed, set the table, put out the napkins, put the pillowcases on the pillows, wipe off the counters, and many other tasks. If you work with them, they consider it all a wonderful game with mommy.

Young children, ages 5 to 11, can be even more help. They can vacuum, wash windows, change beds, do dishes, take out the garbage, and make simple meals. They can also help their siblings, both younger and older, with various other tasks. They are generally still fairly cooperative at this age; the teenage hormones haven't attacked as yet!

Teenagers are a breed unto themselves, but they can be a joy as well as a headache. Teens should move quickly to totally taking care of themselves, for they are in training for entering the outside world. We can expect a lot from them, and if these expectations are cushioned with genuine interest, laughter, and love, we can get what we expect. Of course, this is easier if they've been taught to do their share from the time they were very small. Teens should take care of all their own laundry, including the washing, drying, and putting away. Many mothers balk at the idea of their teenage sons' doing their own laundry, but after their initial reaction of dismay, they grant that the folded underwear they gently lay in their sons' rooms usually stays exactly where they put it—until it ends up dirty, on the floor. "He doesn't care; why should I?" one disillusioned mother finally conceded. Let him take care of himself. When he gets tired of wearing dirty underwear, he'll wash it. Explain the buttons on the machine and leave it to his imagination.

TIPS FOR COOPERATION

It seems obvious that the more children you have, the more work you have to do. A little less obvious is another truth: The more children you have, the more *help* you have. Some women have a regular work team; all it takes, they say, is a strong hand and a little organization. "Ah, but you don't know *my* kids!" is a frequent response to this claim. True, all children are different, but there are some tried and tested techniques for gaining the cooperation of your offspring. They won't work in all cases (nothing does), but consider the following tips that have worked for many women:

1. Give the children a chance to participate in the planning of the chores. Have a regular meeting for this purpose or at least go over the plans as the seasons (and jobs) change. First of all, discuss the jobs that can be eliminated or simplified. Find the easiest way to do things and identify the person in the household best qualified and most inclined to do each job. Let the children communicate and talk openly.

Be certain to use this time (and other times) to share other concerns and interests. This allows each family member to gain a better understanding of the trials and tribulations of those he or she lives with. Mother should be particularly certain to share her thoughts, since she is asking that the children take over a lot of duties many people believe are her job. Make certain the members of your family realize that your work is important and demanding; let them know you're busy and need their assistance.

2. Define exactly what jobs need to be done. Be specific with your description and the standards you expect. The children can't be blamed for doing their tasks incorrectly if you weren't clear about what they were supposed to do. Also, find the time required to show them how to do things right.

3. List the tasks, particularly for younger children. A list has a viewable end, and this bottom line proves that the work will be finished at some point.

4. Be flexible concerning the time a job is done. It's inconsiderate and destructive to demand that the vacuuming be done right after school when you know baseball practice is scheduled at that time. Give general time frames; help them identify specific times if they have trouble figuring it out for themselves.

5. Rotate chores whenever possible. This keeps boring jobs from being quite so boring. It also more equitably distributes the work. Boys can and should do "girl's work," and vice versa.

6. Resist, at all cost, the temptation to do it yourself. Sometimes this seems to be the best solution; many times, it is certainly the easiest. But once you've taken over a task, it's yours. It will be even more difficult to gain help the next time you try.

7. Relax and be generous with praise. We discussed this earlier, but it is so important, it's worth repeating. It's so easy to complain when a job is incomplete. It's more fun, yet easier to forget, to say "thank you" when the children perform their duties well.

PAYING YOUR CHILDREN FOR WORK

There are pros and cons to the issue of paying for chores. Many parents feel children should do chores simply because they're part of the family. On the other hand, they should also share in the wealth of the family. Additionally, children should be taught the value of money, and there's no better way than having some of it! I believe the difference is in the approach you take when moving the money from your hands to theirs.

Some parents routinely give their children an allowance each week. This allowance doesn't have to be directly connected to specific chores, although it frequently is. It can be considered unrelated, although the child is expected to perform certain duties around the house.

Other parents find it more efficient and effective to pay directly. It saves a lot of nag time. You either do it, or you don't. This teaches children to perform for money, but many parents would argue that that's what we all do anyway.

When my stepson was 14, I devised a plan that seemed to work well. We established a list of daily duties I expected him to do. These duties included both the regular items expected of a 14 year old as well as laundry and a job I particularly hated—doing the evening dishes (not just the plates but the pots and pans as well!). Before he went to bed each night, all these jobs had to be done. If they were, I initialed a small, booklike calendar for that day. At first, I checked to see that he had actually completed all tasks. Later I began taking his word for it. (Eventually, we developed a demerit system if I found a "completed" job wasn't really done after all.) On Friday night, he received $2 for each initial. This totaled more money than most boys his age were getting for an allowance, but he was doing more than most of his friends. There was no "makeup" on Tuesday night if he failed to get his initial on Monday. I never asked him if everything was finished, and if he went to bed without getting his booklet checked off, too bad. If he left the dishes in the sink, I left them, too. On Tuesday, he'd have to do Monday's dishes as well as Tuesday's to get the Tuesday initial. All in all, it worked very well. He'd occasionally get angry if he "forgot" to do his work one night and complain it wasn't fair that he had to do double work the next night for the same amount of money, but I stuck to the original plan. It freed me from picking up after him, begging him to do the dishes, asking him to put the toothpaste away, and so forth. I also took him out to dinner on the night the local cafeteria offered its all-you-can-eat weekly specials. This gave us a good chance to talk—and relieved him of his K.P. duties for an evening.

Familial respect is certain to develop when you work as a family to share the work of a family. Everyone learns that it's tough work, but it's work that must be done. They share a greater understanding of what it means to keep a household going; it also provides an opportunity for positive communication as you do the planned work together.

Marge Butler, a 44-year-old insurance coordinator from Wisconsin, is also the mother of four children—a girl, 18, and three boys, 20, 21, and 25. Marge's approach seems to exemplify a smooth-running, busy household of a working woman. I think we all can take some tips from Marge:

> When I hear some of my friends, peers, etc., talk about going home from work and doing the wash and ironing, or spending Saturday cleaning house, and I know they have several children living at home, I get very irritated. They are not only doing themselves a disservice by not getting some help out of these kids; they are also doing the kids a disservice.
>
> My husband and I both grew up on a farm, and he loves to work outside. I'm an indoor person and would be just as happy in an apartment. However, we have a five-bedroom house on a ½-acre lot with lots of yard work and a big vegetable garden every summer. My husband takes care of the outside, because that is his choice. He also does any necessary handy work, such as electrical, plumbing, remodeling, and services our three cars.
>
> I have always worked full-time, even when the children were babies. I have to admit, they were pretty much raised by a baby-sitter. For some people, this wouldn't work; for us, it did. Even if I had been home with my kids, I am not the kind of mother who would have spent time playing with them; that's just not me. My children have developed a sense of independence and responsibility. It has been to their advantage as they grew older.
>
> Of course, all children need spending money, and I suppose every family has what they feel is the best approach to handling that problem; whether it be a weekly allowance or whatever. Because my husband and I

did not receive allowances when we were children, we agreed that our children should have a weekly allowance. At various periods in time, our rules on the allowances were changed, such as whether they were to buy any necessities or if the allowance was just spending money. Because we paid the allowance, and because we were not home all day, and the kids were there more than we were and were the ones to mess it up, I soon decided there was no reason why I should spend the weekend cleaning house, washing, ironing, and cooking. After all, I brought home a substantial paycheck that certainly added to their conveniences, and the definition of *mother* does not include the word *slave*. So, various chores were assigned, and the allowance became their weekly pay for doing some work.

I guess sometime after this arrangement began, I came to the decision that I was not superwoman. For a few years when the children were in school, I was working 50 hours and more per week. My husband worked a lot of overtime, too. Even though the kids were now in charge of cleaning the house and doing the wash and ironing, it wasn't always the way I wanted it. I found myself doing things over and doing a lot of hollering about doing a better job. Well, sometime during this period, it occurred to me that everything didn't have to be perfect all the time, and it was not my sole responsibility to see that it was. After all, we were a family of six people and various pets. If people who came to visit felt uncomfortable because our home looked lived in and wasn't ready for unexpected guests, then they didn't have to come. I didn't have to be a perfect homemaker, mother, and career woman.

And indeed, I had come to realize that I wanted to be a career woman first. I encountered no opposition from the family as far as housework. Whether they agreed that I should be a career woman, I'm not sure. They knew I was happier that way, but maybe they were making some concessions I didn't know about.

The "guilties"? Yes, I've had them. Not about working, but more about doing what I wanted to do, which includes not only working, but membership in a couple of professional organizations and doing some out-of-town traveling. And the fact that the help from the kids has been mostly housework and not much in the way of helping their dad with the outside work. Not necessarily because I already had them so busy working in the house, but more because he does not have the rapport and the talent for gaining their cooperation.

We now have only the two youngest still living at home. They do all the household chores formerly shared by four of them. They are both students and do not have any other jobs. I have encouraged the children to be involved in extracurricular activities in school, and our home has always been open for them to bring their friends over. Consequently, each one of them has developed their own little network of friends and activities.

If you are going to be a working spouse (either one), your employer is entitled to your presence and productivity. Your family must respect your responsibility to your job. Of course, that doesn't just happen; it requires good communication among family members to develop a workable arrangement.

Marge is clearly a take-charge woman who knows how to get things done. She is probably as successful at work as she is at home. Organization, attitude, and communication are important keys—keys Marge has obviously learned to use.

QUALITY TIME AND QUANTITY OF TIME

Every now and then I happen to catch a very special scene on television. The scene is of a family enjoying a night of music together. Mom is at the piano, dad is on the cello, sister plays the violin, and brother plays the bass fiddle. It looks so idyllic, particularly when the other channels are all showing infidelities, arguments, rapes, and murders. I envy people who have such family nights. It looks so fun and happy. It's easy to forget that many years of hard work would have to go into making such an evening possible.

I don't believe such evenings are impossible, however. As we all continue to find more and more demands upon our time, such family times together are increasingly important. A family music night is only one way a family can spend time together, and a well-practiced quartet is only one version of a music night. The important point is planned quality time together.

The term *quality time* is inevitable in a book for working women. There is such a limited amount of actual time that we must make every minute worth more than its real duration. The term *quality time* is usually used to identify the hours we spend with our families; we defend ourselves against the accusations that we are not giving enough time to our primary group by claiming that quality time is better than a greater quantity of time. What does this all mean, really?

I put this question to a single, 43-year-old mother of a teenage son. Olivia Davis is also a former teacher and currently an elementary school principal in Oregon. As a mother and a school principal, Olivia has had ample opportunity to consider the difference between quality and quantity. She makes these comments:

> Quality time is time that is valuable to the person(s) involved. Quality time for my son should be of value to him. Taking time to listen, being involved in activities, sharing our lives are great quality times. I need to

know how he feels, help him understand his own feelings, share his ups and downs, without making judgments. I need to let him know I understand the feelings expressed and avoid telling him not to feel that way.

Quantity time is time we spend when I may be engaged in an activity not related to anything of interest to him. Shopping, being home together, working in the yard, etc., is time that may be valuable to me, but he feels it doesn't count because it isn't important to him, his needs, and feelings. It's a matter of perspective.

There is value to a quantity of time versus quality because it has the potential of becoming valuable. I think we need both. I believe quantity can never make up for quality, but the reverse can be true. We may not have lots of time together, but the short times, if they are valuable and meaningful to him, can compensate for the time we are not able to be together.

If I know in advance that my commitments require me to be away from him, I can plan for some quality time to see us through my busy schedule. He needs to know he is a priority of mine—that I still care, even though he is sharing me with others. It is easy to get so wrapped up in my professional obligations that I can forget to take time to be a mom.

I believe many of us fool ourselves with the issue of quality and quantity. We get so busy being defensive concerning our children that we truly believe any time we spend with them is quality time. Rereading Olivia's definitions can make you realize this is not true.

I discovered this a short time ago. I love to take my five year old out to dinner, just the two of us, assuming this is quality time together. But frequently I take along the evening newspaper, a magazine, or a report to read while we're waiting for our order. She's learned to take along crayons and a book to color, occupying herself while I read.

A few weeks ago, however, I realized I should be ashamed of myself. I had just read Olivia's statement, "quality time is time that is valuable to the person(s) involved," when, evening paper in hand, I picked Jennifer up from school. We headed to an early dinner, and as soon as the waitress had taken our order, I began reviewing the headlines. I noticed Jennifer's little face over the reports of war in the Middle East. "Mommy," she said, "why can't you just talk to *me*?"

Of course, I put the paper down immediately. We talked about school, her teacher, her dinner, her dolls. She laughed and giggled. I laughed, too, but was consumed with shame because I hadn't realized she'd know the difference between "quality time" and "quantity time."

My conscience is eased a little because I know I'm not the only working mother who plays these tricks (although most aren't news junkies like I am!). We get so involved in major issues we believe are important that we can forget about the people in our lives who *are* important and in whose lives we can really make a difference. It's sometimes difficult to be engrossed in your children's interests, but it's a difficulty we must overcome, because the children themselves are important. We can't expect them to understand or appreciate all we're interested in (although we should share as much as possible), so it is our responsibility as the older and "wiser" party to do the bending.

Open communication is central to quality family time. Communication—usually the lack of it—is frequently the main culprit in all family problems. The more people you have in your household, the greater the chance that these communication lines will become tangled, for every additional person in a household geometrically increases the number of communication channels. The formula for the possible number of communications is $N(N - 1)$. It works this way:

In a 2-person household:
$$N(N - 1)$$
$$2(2 - 1) = 2 \times 1 = 2 \text{ communication channels}$$

In a 3-person household
$$N(N - 1)$$
$$3(3 - 1) = 3 \times 2 = 6 \text{ communication channels}$$

In a 4-person household:
$$N(N - 1)$$
$$4(4 - 1) = 4 \times 3 = 12 \text{ communication channels}$$

In an 8-person household:
$$N(N - 1)$$
$$8(8 - 1) = 8 \times 7 = 56 \text{ communication channels}$$

In a family of eight members, there's a good chance of miscommunication with so many relationships. Keeping communications clear and positive is difficult with any number of family members, however, and requires hard work and planning. Hard work and planning are the only way to truly gain that quality time we all desire. Olivia makes the point this way:

These things [quality-time activities] don't just happen unless I plan for them. I can make excuses, blame everything and everybody, but the bottom line is I am in control of my life and can make things happen if they are my priority. Being aware and consistent is one of the biggest hurdles I have to overcome. When things get out of focus, it becomes obvious my priorities were out of whack. So we regroup and start all over again with our lives.

MAKING THE MOST OF THE TIME YOU HAVE

Planning time together is the only way. Before planning, however, determine what activities are worthwhile to you, your children, and your spouse. Once you know what your priorities are, *make* time in your schedule. Don't worry if it interferes with something else you thought you wanted to do; the chances are very good your family *will* interfere. You're left with the old priority question: "Which activity is more important?"

Here are some ideas you can discuss with members of your family. Try to implement one of these new ideas immediately. Remember: The children won't stand still; they are getting older—and farther away from you— each year.

1. Develop the habit of checking in with each other when someone leaves or comes home. Acknowledge each other instead of just hearing the door slam.

2. Develop a regular play time with children; let them choose the game they want to play. Don't watch television while playing; leave the time open for any thoughts they might have to share.

3. Develop a warm time together with young children at bedtime. Read to them; tell stories; sing them to sleep.

4. Share a hobby or sport with your children. If you don't have one currently, develop one together. (I began taking piano lessons when my daughter did. My son also takes piano. We may never become the quartet of my dreams—with dad on the bongos—but we may become the world's first piano trio!)

5. Go for long walks together after dinner. It's good exercise and a wonderful opportunity for easy conversation.

6. Prepare dinner together; eat together; clean up together. Make it a rule that everyone stays in the room, focused on each other and the meal, until the last dish is put away.

7. Write to each other. Develop a joint interest in a controversial subject, write your individual thoughts as you have them, share them with each other.

8. Institute an inviolable family night once a week. Make it a truly important evening. There are many ways you can focus the evening: Show each other how to do something; share some favorite music; join in a service project in the neighborhood; put together a puzzle; share prominent stories from your childhoods; go to a play; make a tape recording of each family member, who shares what is most important in his or her life at any one time; and so on. Be certain the family night *involves* the family members and encourages each person to communicate with the other. Television truly doesn't count as a family activity. When we realize that

the TV is on nearly eight hours a day in most American households, we can be certain there is a quantity of time that is waiting for that special desire to turn it into quality.

The compromises we make to have a family life and a professional life involve many difficult choices. Most of us are continually uncomfortable with the sacrifices we are forced to make on both fronts. Proper planning, however, can help us make the most of the time we have. We and our children also profit from an objective attitude toward mother, which frees us from some of the suffocating demands of the traditional role. We can relax a little when we realize our job is to make our children independent of us instead of dependent on us. It is crucial that we make time with our children an important priority, for no other success can compensate for failure in this important area.

9

FRIENDS AND COMMUNITY

OR

A woman's place is in the home, you know

The conflicts a woman faces go far beyond her job, her home, or her family. Her extended family and the community and world she lives in are a major influence in determining her level of happiness in her job and in her home. Today there are myriad life-styles open to a woman: She can choose to marry or not to marry; she can choose to have children or not to have children; she can choose to work outside the home or not to work outside the home. We cannot abstain from making a choice, and once we choose, there seems to be a need to defend our choice against all other choices.

No conflict is more heated than the war between the working mothers and the stay-at-home mothers. Positions seem to have polarized, and the forces have dug trenches for a long and bitter battle. The issue of quality child care has become the battleground for this fight, which is probably more about chosen life-styles than it is about the needs of children, although many women will not admit it.

We have become quite skilled at hurting each other. Stay-at-homers accuse working women of being money hungry: "The world would be a safer place if only these women would stay at home and raise quality children." The working mothers are just as defensive, contending that all the daytime mothers are wasting their time and talents on trivia. We don't seem to be very empathetic or understanding concerning other life-styles.

Perhaps we're defensive because we're not totally confident we've made the right choice ourselves.

Fortunately, the antagonism abates somewhat once a woman's children are grown. Then a job outside the home may make some sense to many traditional critics, particularly if the woman is helping put the kids through college or working for some other noble reason. Still, many people believe "A woman's place is in the home, you know!" The twenty-first century simply has not arrived in many towns. Let's take a look at some of the influences on a woman's life beyond her immediate circle.

EXTENDED FAMILY

The family beyond the nuclear group can play an important role in helping or hindering the working woman. The extended family can be a valuable source of stability for everyone—children, parents, and grandparents. It provides a sense of identity; we know who we are. We can see other forms of ourselves in our relatives. We can see where we've been through our nieces and nephews, as well as through our children. We continue to reflect and compare ourselves with our siblings throughout our adult life, much as we did as children; this can be a stabilizing influence now as well as then. We understand more about ourselves as we watch our parents grow older, and we gain a richer perspective as we view the scope of life, from our infants to our grandparents. Although this extended family can be difficult to live with, it provides us with an important sense of ourselves.

There are both pros and cons to living in the same city with most of your relatives. On the plus side, they can provide emotional as well as practical support at all times. Grandparents can be an extremely important source of information and help with children. They can relieve their children from the constant pressures of child rearing, gaining and giving immeasurably from having their grandchildren with them.

In some instances, the grandparents have a clearer insight into the problems of their grandchildren than the children's parents have. In fact, there are some suggestions that personality types skip generations; thus, a mild-mannered parent will spawn fiery hot-tempered offspring. Twenty-five years later, the fiery offspring will be surprised to find his or her child more like the grandparent than the parent. This thought adds some meaning to the wry comment, "Grandparents and grandchildren are often good friends because they have a common enemy!"

Many working women have happily used their mothers to help with their children while they work. There's a certain peace of mind to leaving your little ones in your mother's hands, particularly if you feel she was a good mother and *if* she is eager to babysit. There's less guilt attached to having grandma watch the kids than there is to another sitter you might hire. The feeling seems to be that grandmother love is second only to mother love, so it's all right to leave them in her care.

Many grandmothers today, however, aren't so eager to raise their grandchildren after they've raised their own children. Women's liberation has also hit the older set, and many women rightfully want to enjoy their later years. Again, open communication is important in sorting out these conflicting needs. If a grandmother really doesn't want to tend to the grandchildren, the working woman would probably be smart to hire another sitter. Forcing mom to help out potentially presents some very difficult problems for everyone. One of the most obvious problems is that she will probably not be very enthused or attentive—and it's difficult to fire a child's grandmother! Be careful ahead of time before you get grandma into the act on a regular basis.

There are also negative aspects to living in close proximity to your family. Some people never grow up as long as they're within a short drive of their mama's home. Many mothers like it this way, although it creates serious difficulties for their adult children. Many adults revert to childish or teenage behavior when they're around their parents; frequently, one parent brings out this behavior more than the other. These childish adults continue to feel more at home in their parents' home than they do in their own. Many marriages have suffered irreparable damage because one or both partners never entirely grew up.

Living close to parents once you've married can also mean there are more than two adults in a marriage. Marital conflict can become a team sport as the woman's family take her side against "the skunk," and the man's family back their boy against "that woman." Unnecessary and unwanted advice can also flow a little more freely when everyone is close at hand. Many couples find themselves in a day-by-day tug-of-war as they compromise between their first families and the family that developed from their marriage. It's difficult and trying for everyone to let go.

The issue of women working adds additional strain to many extended-family situations. Feelings run strong on this issue, and nowhere do they run stronger than between generations. The common conflict today seems to be that the older generation feels a woman should stay at home and keep house, particularly if she has children. Antagonisms can run for years if this issue is not resolved. The conflict is difficult when a woman's own parents are against her chosen life. The best (and only) help in this situation is a supportive husband—and cotton in the ears.

We can choose to never visit the in-laws, of course, but that step is a little childish and extreme; his parents are probably still important to their child, as well as meaningful to our own children. Through the years, you can get used to in-law hassles; women have been doing it for generations, only on different issues. The issue of work is only the most recent point of contention, and it won't be the last.

Try to realize that all families have problems; yours is no different. Many of us believe our brother's daughter is too loud, or our sister's teen-age son is too wild, or cousin Mary is nothing but a gossipy old bore, or Harry's wife makes a terrible stew. This is all part of the fun and games of extended family life. It can be fun if we let it be—and if we find a way to learn from and grow in response to those who are very much like us (really!), yet so very different.

YOUR CIRCLE OF FRIENDS

We are more comfortable with friends who are like ourselves. We tend to seek them out to reaffirm that we're O.K. people. There's little wrong with this, and it does seem to be true that birds of a feather flock together.

During the first year we dated, my husband and I used to enjoy playing an interesting guessing game. We were graduate students and lived in an all-graduate dormitory on campus. The average age of the students in that dorm was 32.

The dining hall was a meeting room, of sorts; it consisted of an ocean of rectangular tables, each seating six to eight students. Twenty-five per-cent of the students in this dorm were foreign students studying at the university.

The dining hall was a wonderful place for people-watching. Even an amateur watcher could quickly identify the patterns. There was a table for the Chinese physicists, the female P.E. majors, the French art majors, the business management students, the ed. psych. majors—you get the pic-ture. Our game was to figure out who was who by the way they walked, talked, and interacted. The devilish way to upset everyone was to sit at one of the "topical" tables and try to talk about something other than The Topic. Most students at these tables would look at you as though you were from Mars. Their eyes told the story: They had absolutely no idea what you were talking about.

The same game is played in the suburbs, in the condos, and in the apartment complexes. We tend to seek out those who are like us, confirm-ing the choices we've made about our lives. We enjoy being comfortable and nonthreatened; forget about the fact that we seldom learn anything new. At least we're secure.

When we are mothers of families, this tendency to flock to your own has additional implications. It's difficult for us personally if we can't find other women with the same perspective as our own. A working woman who lives in a predominantly traditional community becomes the creature from Mars; on the other hand, a stay-at-home mother who lives on a street where all the other mothers work becomes the oddity on her block. The feeling is a very strange one and cannot be brushed off as easily as we might hope. It is difficult to truly feel that everyone has a right to live the way she chooses. There is not usually open hostility toward the "ugly duckling"; there is only an indefinable thick air between the woman and her neighbors.

Adding to the pressures of this uncomfortable situation is the fact that husbands and (particularly) children compare their wives/mothers. "Tommy's mother goes to *all* his ballgames" and "Why don't you cook the way Sandy's mom cooks?" can be very bothersome quips. "Why don't you do something, mom?" or "Why don't you dress the way Barb's mother dresses?" can be equally painful. When our families are important to us, their comments about us make an impression. We want them to be proud of us, no matter what we do, but we're not always ready to make the personal sacrifice to gain their approval. We can try to explain the value of choice in today's world; we can stress that different people have different needs; we can point out the advantages we have because we work (or don't work); we can hope our child understands. The children probably won't understand, and many of them will soon forget they even asked the question. Their mother, however, is often left with an additional set of guilt complexes.

Again, a little backbone is in order. Of course, your children won't have exactly the same life they'd have if you stayed home 95 percent of the time, but they *will* have different experiences, most of which will prove beneficial to them. Concentrate on the positive aspects of your employment. Always stress the positive aspect of any situation, no matter how difficult it is to find.

Whenever possible, you may want to seek your own support group, even if you have to look outside your neighborhood, subdivision, or city to find it. Within a town of any size there are "life-style pockets." A 20-minute drive can provide you with a totally different (and more familiar) picture of living. If you feel in need of meeting more people like you, don't be afraid to look for them. They will provide you with new confidence when you are back home.

THE LOSS OF A FRIEND

Different life-styles can appeal to different people at different times. Just because you lived a certain way in 1975 doesn't mean you'll live that same way in 1985. Needs change; finances may become a problem; personal goals may shift; strange desires may find their time. When any of these events occur, we are likely to take action—and become someone new. It hurts a great deal when that person was our best friend, who shared both heartaches and victories during some very important times.

Pam was such a friend to me. We met at a most traumatic time in my life: My father had just died; my husband had changed jobs; we moved to Michigan; I was forced to leave the doctoral program and university teaching responsibilities I loved; and I was pregnant for the first time at 31. I felt stifled and forced into the role of traditional woman.

Pam was in her middle thirties, had been home raising two children for almost 15 years, and was aching to get back in the "real" world. We liked each other a great deal from the moment we met. It proved to be an important friendship for both of us.

Pam helped me toward the motherhood role I had long avoided. We talked for hours over lunch; our conversation centered on traditional women's topics for the first time in my life. I had no job, no outlet, and was definitely pregnant.

I helped Pam gain the confidence and direction she needed to move outside the home, back into the career of her dreams. She was totally unsure of herself; the biography she wrote for the graduate school application sounded more like an apology for living than a description of her life.

She filled me in on the details of giving birth, nursing, and raising babies; I showed her how to write a good application, find money, and organize her household to be more independent of her. We were both very helpful to the other; our paths had crossed, in the truest sense of the word, as we, in a way, switched roles.

For a year or so, I thought we had both been too helpful. Pam was soon at the top of her class in graduate school and moved on to a prominent teaching and counseling position in our community within a few short years. My apprehensions concerning motherhood disappeared the moment I saw my baby, and I was quickly back in the swing of things, moving on to a new aspect of my career. But I still wanted to share with Pam; she was the best friend I had ever had.

It took me some time to realize she really didn't want to see me. I was always the one to call to set up a luncheon date; she was never available. After four invitations were turned down, I decided that *she* must initiate the get-together, not me. She said she would, but the phone never rang.

I was hurt and confused. Had I said something wrong? Had I not said something I should have? What happened?

One day, a couple of years later, I saw her in the shopping center. I hesitated before calling out her name, but then I quietly said, "Pam." She looked startled, but happy. I was uncertain as she pulled out her date book and gave me two alternative dates. We met for lunch two weeks later, and I'm glad we did. I'm no longer hurt and disappointed.

I figured a few things out after talking with Pam, one final time. (I heard she's moved to another city now.) All friendships, perhaps the best friendships, don't have to last forever. People change—and change rapidly—in today's world. The Pam I finally met for lunch was a totally different person from the insecure housewife I had known in 1976. Of course, I was a totally different person, too. We had a love between us back then that was based on need, and our needs were met. Each of us had continued to grow; this growth meant we grew away from each other. Our friendship was good for the time we shared it and is still an important memory, but it no longer would have any meaning. I sincerely hope she has new friends who are adding to her life in the same way we added to each other's lives. If our friendship had remained stagnant, perhaps we would still be friends, talking about the same issues with slightly different words. If this were the alternative, the price would be too high.

We lose friends when we change. The loss doesn't diminish the friendship as it existed, but that doesn't make the loss any easier to accept. When you move on to a new challenge in your life, all things about your life, habits, and friendships are likely to change. There's a chain reaction whenever you change one aspect. Some friendships adjust and adapt to the new circumstances; others do not. We're lucky new doors are always opened to us once an old door is closed.

BEYOND THE COMMUNITY: THE WAY IT IS

The popular approach to a discussion of women's issues is to be open-minded and noncommittal. We frequently hear statements such as, "Of course, it's up to each woman to decide for herself what she wants. It's a free country. The important thing is that every woman should do what she wants to do without feeling guilty!"

This statement offends no one and makes everyone comfortable with her own personal choice. It's a politician's statement—good if you're running for office, but it says nothing. Of course, women will continue to seek the life they want to live. The homemakers will dream of and search for a man with potential and try to turn him into a good husband and father. The career-minded women will go on finding their way in the business world; most of them will eventually try to combine family life with their professional aspirations. Each type of woman will defend her choice more strongly as the years go by, causing friction and tensions between all women. Still, the choice is theirs to make.

Unfortunately, from a practical standpoint, I no longer believe we have much of a choice. The handwriting is on the wall, and it is quite clear, no matter how many women want to bury their heads in the sand and ignore it. For our own sake and for the sake of our children (those now living and those yet to be born), women *must* choose to engage in some form of employment or career. If we want to earn our fair share from that career, we must plan carefully and give it serious attention; to do otherwise is almost self-destructive.

Despite the fact that the Equal Pay Act of 1963 guaranteed equal pay for equal work, most women still earn relatively little when compared to their male counterparts. According to Labor Department statistics, a woman employed full-time earned an average of $224 per week in 1981; a man employed full-time earned $347 per week. This is a 35.5 percent difference in pay. Statisticians used to rationalize that this difference reflected the lack of experience most women suffer from; this assumption, however, has not explained it. These figures are for men and women in the same occupations.

Evidence that women are the "nouveau poor" in the United States is also shown in these figures:

90 percent of all people receiving minimum Social Security benefits are women.

60 percent of those on Medicare are women.

69 percent of food stamps recipients are women.

80 percent of those receiving aid to families with dependent children are women.

75 percent of Americans living below the poverty level are women.

These frightening statistics are explained in large measure by women who bought the Cinderella dream. They planned to marry a young man they loved, have children, and live happily ever after while daddy went off to work to earn the living and they (the mommy) stayed home to tend the hearth. The only problem is the fairy tale had a surprise ending for many women. They were unexpectedly cut off from their financial support through the disappearance of their husbands.

There's even a new name for these women: displaced homemakers. The Displaced Homemakers Network in Washington, D.C., estimates there are over *4 million* displaced homemakers in this country. *Displaced home-maker* is defined as "someone whose primary source of income is lost through death, divorce, or desertion, and this person has no marketable skills." To grasp the severity of the problem consider this: The number of households headed by a lone woman with kids under the age of 18 jumped 97.1 percent (to 5.6 million) between 1970 and 1981. The picture is clear: In some cases, the men are dying at an earlier age, but more frequently the men are taking their incomes with them as they leave their wives and children to fend for themselves. Alimony and child support? Almost nonexistent. If a woman is lucky, she can expect her ex-husband to help support her and their children for a few years. After that, she's on her own.

It's difficult to consider these startling statistics without becoming cynical toward all men. No one really wants to mistrust all men: It's not fair, because they're *not* all alike, and it's not beneficial for either sex to be mistrusting of the other. Some men have a cynical view of women, too, as expressed in the following condensed version of a letter to the editor of a large city newspaper that had recently printed a story about a (formerly) upper-middle-class woman and her three children who had been abandoned by their husband/father:

> My experience has been a woman uses her sexual characteristics to entice a man into a sexual relationship and then a binding marital contract. If he fails to satisfy her, it's off to the divorce lawyer, who will then aid her in her efforts to strip her ex-husband of a substantial portion of his income and all his pride and masculinity. The legal system has made it easier for a woman to make a living from her ex-husband than from producing a product or service for the marketplace and thus be faced with the realities men must face for life.

Admittedly, this assessment may be true *in some cases*. I do not believe, however, that it honestly portrays the reality of most divorces. Whenever there is a dependency relationship between two people, there is bound to be a feeling that one is taking advantage of the other. As human beings, we tend to see any situation better from our own perspective, emphasizing our own disappointments and heartaches. Of course, there are many "hurts" in any divorce; the point is, when the marriage was based on traditional roles, the male takes the money with him when he leaves. The female, frequently lacking the skills necessary to secure a decent position, is forced to find a source of support for herself and her children. Naturally, she turns to the sire of her children; she has been taught that he would take care of her and their children "until death do us part."

We all want to believe our husbands will love us forever and stand by us. The men usually begin with the same expectations of their wives. But times, circumstances, fortunes, and personalities change. The way things were this year is not the way things will be next year. We are all vulnerable, and in the final analysis, we are all responsible for ourselves.

Many of the working women today are not working by choice but because they found themselves in exactly the situation described above. They had to take what they could get, for their own survival and for the survival of their children. Some men are beginning to fight for custody of their children. These child-custody fights are increasingly won by the man, whose experience, money, and connections give him access to better lawyers to fight his battle.

In some cases, of course, the father is the better parent. Some women, like some men, choose to seek personal fulfillment at the expense of their families. They leave their children in the hands of their husbands to "find themselves." But there is a very important difference. Although these women hurt their families deeply when they leave, they usually don't take the family's major earning power with them. Their former husbands may have a difficult time when faced with their ex-wives' abandoned responsibilities, but the men are more likely to have the ability to earn money for their families. Their children will eat and be clothed—off the welfare rolls.

Of course, we don't want to think of these possibilities on our wedding day. We prefer to believe our love is different and we won't get caught. Unfortunately, statistics show that over 50 percent of all marriages will not make it "till death do us part." This 50 percent figure is likely to rise even higher, as respected social researcher Daniel Yankelovich states: "Surveys reveal the virtual abandonment of some our mostly deeply held beliefs about family and marriage."*

I am not advocating that women go to war with men or refuse to marry. Men, in many ways, are as much the victims as we are. I *am* suggesting that we separate love from financial dependency. This means women go to work. This will eventually give men greater freedom as well. Hopefully, this will bring more and more couples to the point of *inter*dependence, greater happiness, and long-lasting marriages.

We have talked throughout this book and throughout our lives of the many conflicts and compromises women are forced to make when they choose to combine a home and family with a career. Perhaps the difficult

* "New Rules in American Life: Searching for Self-Fulfillment in a World Turned Upside Down," *Psychology Today*, April 1981.

choices will be a little easier once we accept the fact that the role of the happy stay-at-home wife and mother is becoming a iuxury of another age. We must learn to balance our homes and our jobs simultaneously, because there is no other reasonable choice. We must plan for the future with reality in our hip pockets. The enactment of this plan will take tears, courage, and commitment, but it's really the only game in town.

PART IV
LOOKING AHEAD

10

WHERE DO WE GO FROM HERE?

What are our choices for the future? We have examined our past, exploring briefly how we arrived at the precarious place where we find ourselves today. We have given close attention to where we are now, analyzing the many conflicts we feel regarding our families, our homes, our communities, and our jobs. We have exhausted some useful ideas for coping with the pressures and demands of our existence as we attempt to integrate two worlds, one outside the home and one inside the home. Some ideas work; others do not. But we make it, we hope, a little better each day.

If we ever really hope for a better deal, for ourselves and for our sons and daughters, though, we must look toward the future. What lies ahead? What can we expect? Let's consider some of the trends.

There will be more people in the labor force than ever before in history. In the year 2000, there will be 31 million people working in the United States, ⅓ more than today. These workers will have an average age 3 years older than the average age of workers today (38 years instead of 35).

There will be more women in this workforce. Fewer and fewer couples will live in the traditional relationship that found the man working outside the home in support of a stay-at-home wife and family. "In 1960," stated a recent article, "43 percent of all households consisted of a married couple with only one spouse in the labor force; by 1975, this had dropped to 25 percent, and by 1990, it is projected to be only 14 percent."* In 1981, 52.3 percent of women over the age of 16 were in the labor force, up from 37.8 percent in 1960. This rise is probably reflective of the trend toward later marriages: The average age at the time of marriage in 1960 was 22.8; in 1980, it was 24.6.†

* *The Grand Rapids Press*, December 13, 1981.
† Bruce Chapman, "How America Will Change in the Next Decade," *U.S. News and World Report*, March 22, 1982, pp. 51–53.

Looking toward the future, I believe all women must assess where they are and, from that point, develop a contingency plan for their own support. This plan should consider their present marital status and financial situation and point them toward their best option in case their situation changed, for any reason. Of course, the older woman has fewer options than the younger woman, but all women should make plans and gain the required skills to care for themselves financially.

This is a somewhat cynical approach, but it is based on reality instead of pipe dreams. I still believe strongly in the institution of marriage, but it will be stronger once we begin separating it from the element of total economic dependency. Statistics show that, despite all the problems we face as women move out of the home and into the workforce, only one in five Americans say they want a return to the traditional housekeeping norms, sex relations, and male monopoly on working outside the home. * Our plans and blueprints for the future must therefore include new ways of organizing our industries that will serve the needs of the changing family and the changing nature of the workforce as we move toward the year 2000. Let's take a look at some of these efforts.

BUSINESS LEARNING TO DEAL WITH WOMEN

Half of all women with children under six years old are in the workforce. This astounding percentage, which promises to grow in the future, has gained the attention of major corporations. Many are now beginning to respond to the needs of these women and their families, according to a report in which 374 corporations and 815 couples were surveyed. These corporations are interested in the needs of the involved families more for practical reasons than for sentimental ones; they see advantages in:

Recruiting: Corporations that pay attention to family needs are rare. Top employees will be drawn by special concessions to families.

Employee morale: Employees work better when their family lives are settled. Contentment on the personal front allows workers to give greater attention to the demands of their jobs.

Productivity and profits: The name of the game is productivity and profits. With happier, more satisfied employees, free to put in a good day's work, these two important "Ps" will increase.

This report, funded by Exxon and conducted in 1980 by Catalyst (a

* "Reducing Stress in Two-Career Families—Expert's Advice," U.S. News and World Report, November 2, 1981, p. 90.

New York-based nonprofit organization that works to develop careers for women in corporate and professional life), found that the corporations surveyed are moving toward a number of useful developments to aid the two-career family. The most important ideas should be explored further. They are:

Flexible work hours and job sharing.
Child-care services.
A "cafeteria" approach to benefits.
Spouses' relocation services.

Let's examine each of these more carefully. Two-career families have much to gain as these services become more widely available.

Flexible Work Hours and Job Sharing

Flexible work hours give employees much more autonomy. The employees are more in charge of their own coming and going, thus permitting them to integrate all sorts of non-work-related activities into their day. With flexible hours, an employee can go to the dentist, meet baby-sitter time requirements, or pick Harry up at the airport in the middle of a weekday afternoon. Flexible hours can also be important merely because they allow the employee some choice, for no reason at all.

Many flextime systems have a "core" time period when all employees are expected to be present. This core time is frequently between 9:00 A.M. and 3:00 P.M. The employee can vary from that base in any way that is convenient. Some may want to work the eight hours from 7:00 A.M. until 3:00 P.M.; others may choose to work from 8:00 to 4:00 or from 9:00 to 5:00. Time clocks record the amount of time spent on the job. Supervisors, of course, are ultimately responsible for the work but are not required to be there at all times. This has the added advantage of encouraging effective delegation from supervisor to employee. Flextime also cuts absenteeism as an employee who might previously have called in sick because of a scheduled dentist's appointment can now honestly work the required hours before breaking for the appointment.

Some companies are discovering the benefits of employing part-time people. Many are finding that two fresh people are better than one person who tends to tire at midday. Part-time employees also frequently suffice to fill a position formerly held by a full-time person, thus saving money and time as well (since a person with nothing to do is a huge timewaster for all others in the workplace).

A slight variation on part-time employment is the relatively new, but growing, idea of job sharing. Job sharing refers to two people sharing the duties, responsibilities, and benefits of one position. This work arrangement (including some part timers) may involve as many as 28 percent of all workers by the year 1990.* Job sharing has special benefits for the employers, for it provides the talents of two people instead of one. Two brains can attack a problem. The strengths of one will likely be utilized in one circumstance, while in another crisis, the other person's skills may be nearer the company's needs. There is little or no absenteeism in job sharing, for there is always a knowledgeable substitute who can take over. The biggest drawback to implementing more job-sharing situations is inertia. Management is hesitant to change because it has seldom been done. How can you go about selling the idea of job sharing to a particular company? Here are some suggestions:

1. Determine the kind of work you really want to do. It's best to be truly "sold" on this job, because you must fight tradition to divide it, and management must feel you are serious about the work you propose to do. You will be more serious if you know what you want.

2. Is the work you want to do as a job sharer the job you already have? If it is, you have a big advantage in getting it reorganized. You know the job well and know how it can be divided. Your dedication has already been established (for better or worse).

3. Itemize the goals, duties, responsibilities, and strains of the job. Dissect it carefully. Match your strengths, likes, and skills to a reasonably organized segment of the job.

4. Find a complementary, compatible second party. This person doesn't have to be exactly like you; in fact, it would be best if he or she weren't skilled in exactly the same areas as you. Talk honestly with each other. Anticipate problems; develop alternative solutions.

5. Carefully detail, on paper, how the job would be split. List the benefits *to the employer* of this arrangement. Include work schedule, responsibilities, and check points for your plan. Be certain to include a financial analysis of the job you propose to share.

6. Think through the lines of communications that should be developed between you, your partner, and your employer before you approach the employer with your idea. Clear communications is the most important ingredient in making job sharing successful.

7. Approach your employer with your carefully developed plan. Be confident and knowledgeable. Anticipate hesitations, but don't become aggressive—or defensive. If you've done your homework and are confident on the basis of your findings, you should have a well-prepared case.

8. Be prepared to accept a trial run for the job. The trial basis is more comfortable for many employers whenever they attempt something new.

* Nancy C. Baker, "Divide and Conquer," *Working Mother*, January 1981, p. 14.

9. When you get the go-ahead, be certain to deliver more than your fair share. Particularly at first, you'll have to go that extra mile to insure success, but it will still be worth the effort. It will also encourage your employer to be more open to other innovative options.

Job sharing doesn't have to be a 50/50 deal, with one person working the 8:00 to 12:00 shift and another person working the 1:00 to 5:00 shift. Some job sharers work Monday/Tuesday/Wednesday morning and Wednesday afternoon/Thursday/Friday. Others work one week on, the next week off. Some work one month on, the next month off. Some agree to a 60/40 or a 75/25 split of responsibilities and benefits. Whatever looks reasonable—and will "fly"—is worth a try. Flexible work hours and shared responsibilities offer many advantages to male and female employees and employers alike.

Child-Care Services

Forward-thinking companies are getting into the child-care business in one way or another. Company planners need only glance at the rapid movement of women into the workforce to realize that the most important problem that will be bothering American two-career families in the future has to do with raising children. Businesses are becoming partners with parents in providing for the children in some very innovative ways.

Some companies have gone to on-site day-care. Fox Chase Medical Center in Philadelphia, Stride Rite in Boston, and PCA International in Charlotte, North Carolina, are only a few of the many companies that have calmed the concerns of their employees who are also parents by establishing child-care facilities on their premises. Children come to work and go home with one or both parents. Some parents join their children for lunch on a regular or occasional basis. They are always nearby, if the need arises. Such aid with child care provides the expected benefits to the company—many of the same benefits encountered through flexible work schedules: reduction in worker turnover, absenteeism, and tardiness; and a corresponding boost in employee morale and dedication. Other child-care ideas include:

- Subsidies to employees based on the need for community day-care facilities.
- A consortium of businesses in one area that collaborate on a day-care facility.
- A child-care information and referral service that matches the child-care needs of employees with good child care in the community.

Cost-effectiveness of any of these programs is a big concern to board-level management. Renee Y. Magid provides some valuable figures that shed a positive light on the cost-effectiveness of such programs.* Magid points out that retirement programs can cost from 8 percent to 10 percent of total direct payroll; basic family dental plans generally range from 1 percent to 1.5 percent of the same payroll base. In contrast to these figures, the child-care program at one company (Fox Chase Medical Center in Philadelphia) is expected to draw .5 percent of direct payroll in first-year operating costs, plus approximately .3 percent of payroll for initial seed money. This is a small price to pay for decreased turnover and increased effectiveness of training.

Careful planning is required to successfully implement a day-care program in any company. Planners should:

1. Determine the need for a child-care program. Survey employees to correctly assess need and interest.
2. Set up a child-care committee to develop the idea further. This committee should include decision-making management, labor representatives, professionals knowledgeable in child-care needs, and public relations specialists.
3. Make a survey of child care already available.
4. Publicize the committee's activities and findings to insure acceptance of its forthcoming actions by both labor and management.
5. Consider hiring outside professionals to help implement the committee's decision.
6. Encourage a positive approach to the new venture, allaying the doubts of the skeptical members of management and the workforce.

Improved child care is the key to improved family relations, which in turn is the key to more productive employees. When the bottom line must be improved productivity, forward-thinking organizations are expanding their former definitions of what they must do to keep their employees happy—and working!

A Cafeteria Approach to Benefits

Health insurance and a week's vacation are no longer enough. Many companies are now turning to the "cafeteria" approach to benefits and incentives for their employees. One package deal is now frequently inadequate to meet the needs of a rapidly changing workforce.

Many companies find a workable balance by offering a core package of

---

* "Parents and Employers: New Partners in Child Care," *Management Review*, March 1982, p. 40.

benefits and then allowing their employees to choose from other fringe benefits, reflecting their needs. The element of choice is a big plus for an employee whose spouse already has medical and dental insurance for the whole family; for this employee, medical and dental benefits would be useless. Felice N. Schwartz, president of Catalyst, reports that 8 percent of 374 corporations surveyed in 1981 offered the cafeteria approach. Approximately 62 percent tended to favor the idea.* This positive response is good news for the future for all two-career families.

Spouses' Relocation Services

Moving has always been traumatic for families, but traditionally, big business had the reputation of not being concerned about the trials and tribulations of family life resulting from corporate moves. Fortunately, this callous attitude appears to be changing as more and more people are refusing to move for family reasons. Promotions are no longer enough incentive. Transfers are particularly difficult when a working spouse must give up his or her job to accommodate the move.

Here's where a spouses' relocation service has been useful. These services aid the employee's spouse in the effort to find a job comparable to or better than the one being vacated by the move. Some corporations are offering the spouse attractive positions in their own companies if they definitely want the family to move. These corporations are forced to make such concessions as the second job now becomes a primary consideration.

The labor force is more complicated when both adult members of a family are employed. Someday, the two-career family will be commonplace, and many of the considerations discussed above will be routine matters. Until that day, when life will be somewhat easier for our children and grandchildren, we must shift and negotiate, compromise and adjust. We must try new systems that will successfully move us toward a better integration of family and professional life.

WOMEN IN MANAGEMENT

In 1980, for the first time in history, there were more females than males in American graduate schools of business.† This fact will have astounding implications for the future of management. Of course, there will be more

---

* "Reducing Stress in Two-Career Families—Expert's Advice," *U.S. News and World Report,* November 2, 1981, p. 90.
†Frank Feather, "The De-Sexing of Management," *Industry Week,* October 5, 1981, p. 15.

and more women entering the management ranks, but these women will also encounter younger men who are more accustomed to working with women—men who are aware that some women are just as competent as some men and that sex has very little to do with a person's ability.

How will management styles change as more and more women enter management? Will managing become more "feminine"? Should it? Or will women try to adopt the management styles of the past, fitting into the "old boy network" by becoming one of the old boys?

The vanguard of women in management have generally tried to emulate men on their road to success. The feeling seemed to be, "If you want to be successful, fashion yourself after a successful person." Unfortunately, there weren't too many successful women; thus, corporate man became the role model. Many women refused to consider that there could be any other way, fearing that pointing to the differences between women and men might lead to the dictum that women were, after all, inferior.

Then, too, the bureaucratic system seems to be based on limited roles, rules, and methods; it is fairly stringent concerning behavior. But the bureaucratic system becomes a little less secure in an uncertain economic climate. Charles Handy, of the London Graduate School of Business Studies, points out the way bureaucratic managers tend to cope with uncertainty. The symptoms are familiar: polarizing problems into black or white, planning for short periods, seeking routine, getting involved in trivia, reacting rather than taking the initiative, flaring up, withdrawing, working harder and longer, writing more reports, holding more meetings, making more visits, escapism through drink or drugs, and eventual breakdowns.* Surely both men and women managers of the future can find better ways of dealing with uncertainty!

There seems to be a strong disagreement about how different women really are from men. As soon as you digest the results of one study that claims women are rather like men, you read in another study about the inborn differences between the male and female human brains.

Jay Hall, president of Taleometrics International, and Susan Donnell, his associate, studied 2,000 male and female managers, looking into five aspects of management behavior. Their conclusion was that there was "no significant difference in the attitudes, approaches, or abilities of the participating men and women."† You can, of course, wonder whether their approaches to management were the same because the female managers had learned to manage by watching male managers, thus acting much like their male counterparts and responding to questions and research as men

*Lou Willet Stanek, "Women in Management: Can It Be a Renaissance for Everybody?" *Management Review*, November 1980, p. 46.
†"Are Women Managers Different from Men?" *Management Review*, December 1980, p. 52.

would. The conclusion of the study, nonetheless, was that "women, in general, do not differ from men, in general, in the ways in which they administer the management process."

Frank Feather, superintendent of domestic regions for the Canadian Imperial Bank of Commerce, cofounder/president of Global Futures network, and director of Global Management Bureau, would tend to disagree with the "women do not differ" approach. Feather stresses that women, through "inborn differences," have much to add to resolving the confusing issues involved in successful management. He points to women's superior verbal skills, abilities in abstract visualization, developed intuition regarding social cues, and the greater flexibility of the female brain. * Even pointing to the advantages females enjoy calls down the wrath of the ardent feminists, who maintain there are no differences.

The nature/nurture aspect of male/female relationships has been analyzed and researched *ad nauseam*; research will continue on this subject, with little chance that much will be resolved. Meanwhile, life goes on. We are left with living and planning our own actions, playing the hand we were dealt and working with the future we plan for ourselves.

A prudent approach to the issue seems to be this:

1. Stress the similarities between men and women instead of the differences.
2. Carefully identify the best qualities in the opposite sex and try to develop those positive qualities in yourself.
3. Use any other personal characteristics, whether generally associated with male or female behavior, to your advantage. Don't suppress the beneficial qualities in yourself that seem to be more "female"; they could provide you with that important edge that marks the difference between success and failure.

Fear of uncertainties seems to be a major problem for everyone as we continue to move toward a greater integration of sex roles. Both men and women feel threatened from many angles. We tend to recoil, retreating to a more secure world with attitudes we believe we understand.

But there is no retreating; looking backward is useless. And we know "the good old days" weren't really all that good, after all; they only seem to be that way because they're behind us and we can understand them a little better than we can understand the future.

Planning, with confidence and clarity, is still the key. As women, we must bring our best with us as we strive to carry an equal share. There are also many benefits for men as the number of female managers continues to increase. The positive integration of males and females works both

* "The De-Sexing of Management," *Industry Week*, October 5, 1981, p. 15.

ways, and men (as many are already discovering) will find their lives en-
riched by the new kind of woman who will be by their side both at home
and on the job front.

TECHNOLOGY IS THE FUTURE

Our future will be a technological one; this there is no denying. In 1975,
when I read that computers would be as much a part of our lives as tele-
visions within ten years, I didn't believe it. Now I do. Most people are
still uncomfortable with the technological invasion, but the successful
people will accept this reality and become excited by the many doors it
opens.

Women and men alike would be smart to develop their skills in logic
in preparation for technological involvement. Word processing requires
that people picture documents in their minds, type blindly, and think
logically. Word processing will also require precision of thought, since
messages will be developed and delivered more frequently through the
printed media instead of by phone or in person. Writing must be clear,
concise, and unambiguous. This, you will note, requires skills many managers currently lack.

Technology will also decentralize the workplace. Employees won't necessarily work in the same building, sharing the same coffeepot. This dis-
persement will call for a new type of management—new for both the
manager and the worker. Home terminals will likely be a part of our future, and more people will work at home. Managers will have to manage
without having their staff under their thumb. Different problems may develop. Will people like working alone? Will they find it more difficult than
ever to be motivated? Will jobs really be eliminated, as many fear?

Getting in on the ground floor of this technological age would be a
good move for anyone. We must grow with this one certainty in an otherwise uncertain future. The more we know about the technology that
will dominate our lives and dictate our success, the more we will be comfortable with it and learn to use it. When we arrive at this peace, technology will become as familiar as the dishwasher, serving us well, instead
of getting in our way.

ON THE HOME FRONT:
TIGHTENING UP AND GOING FORWARD

What will the future of the family look like? It depends whose crystal ball
you use. Some see the demise of the family, reasonably assuming that the

focus on the individual is contrary to the concept of sharing and compromising demanded by family life. Some see the family as a relic of the past, needed for survival in yesteryear, but an antiquated institution in our chrome-plated future.

Betty Friedan, however, earned the wrath of many radical feminists when she published her book *The Second Stage* in 1981. The author of the 1963 landmark book *The Feminine Mystique*, Friedan moved forward to the point of including men, marriage, and a family in her vision of the future for women. To the charges that she has sold out to the male and female conservative right, Friedan responds:

> Some militants repudiated all the parts of the personhood of women that have been and are still expressed in family, home, and love. In trying to ape men's lives, they have truncated themselves away from grounding experiences. If young women lock themselves into the roles of ambitious men, I'm not sure it's a good bargain. It can be terribly imprisoning and life-denying. *

Other militant women agree with her. Tania Harvey, a 26-year-old self-proclaimed feminist who works in a women's center, shares insights into her marriage, a marriage that differs dramatically from our memories of matrimony as it was 50 years ago:

> I have been married for a year and a half to a man I have known for four years and lived with for three. As a feminist, I know that the institution of marriage has been oppressive for many women. And so I question its presence in my life. I chose to marry out of love. My relationship with Harry is not primarily a passionate one of the heart (although we have our passionate times). I knew that H was a good person, a good person for me to be with, that we had a lot of the same values and goals, that we had compatible interpersonal styles and creative problem-solving processes. I have been able to work on a lot of my own personal issues and make a lot of personal/psychological growth through my union with H. This might sound really heady, but I believe we are all born into the world with certain challenges to work on. My challenge has been to accept the feminine in myself (in the Jungian sense of dependence, vulnerability, intuition, and sensitivity) and blend this into a healthy union with my masculine side (decisive, confident, task and action orientation). My union with H has allowed me to make such progress along these lines.
>
> I am also a conscious person—consciously seeking answers to certain questions. Harry is a conscious person, too. I believe we have been able to reach new/deeper levels of truth through conscious effort. I think being

* Quoted in an interview by Nan Robertson of *The New York Times*, published as "For Friedan, Feminism's Future Includes Men and Kids," *Detroit Free Press*, October 27, 1981, p. 3B.

married helps with this in that we have more commitment to working on issues now than when we were not legally tied. This is part of what marriage meant to us. So far, for me, being married to H has been worth it.

With women in my work life, I have consciously decided not to pursue any (sexual) temptations with them. (Hope this is not too shocking for you. Your questions assumed a heterosexual bias that I'm ignoring in an attempt to be honest.) This was not an easy decision. I opened my heart, asked myself a bunch of questions, and made a decision which I believe to be the right decision for me at this time in my life.

Other men: I have been tempted. I have followed my desire to have one man in an intimate part of my life. This union has been a passionate/ wonderful addition to my life. I have learned many things and felt new joy and inspiration. I held this spark in my arms and transmitted it to others. I did some honest looking at my primary relationship (with H) and have made some positive changes in it. Through my passionate relationship with T (this is a relationship of the heart, soul, and body), I have learned more about my needs and was able to express these needs in my primary relationship and have them met. Neat. I also experienced new depths of pain with H. Scary—very scary. But in some ways very exciting. I have new confidence in the strength of our union. I know we can weather difficult times. The issue is not resolved; it is still fraught with unsettled questions. I feel as if I must choose between my heart and my mind, and I'm not willing to sever myself so. I also know that being with T has some definitely negative influences on my life with H, and I don't want that. I feel this is a challenge: What kind of concessions/compromises am I willing to make through my desire to forge a healthy union with H?

I want to have a child or two when I'm able to afford a nanny. I can't imagine caring for a crying, screaming, messy infant. There are too many things I want to accomplish in my life to make the commitment to raise a child or two. My perspective on this has changed some in the last few years. I can see that in a few years, I might choose to bring child(ren) into my life. Have to learn how to change diapers and how to talk to kids. Need to work on getting myself, career, and union in better shape before adding kids to the picture. If then. I'm not very mature or realistic about having kids so far. If I had a child who wasn't a feminist and didn't adore playing tennis, I'd be very unhappy.

I have shared Harvey's thoughts at length because I found them most revealing and insightful. I believe she expresses well the feelings of many ambitious women today. She does not reflect all thoughts, of course, but she does provide a good yardstick for measuring our own shifting mores and ideas as our whole approach to work, marriage, and the family changes. In many ways, she is Elizabeth Cady Stanton 150 years later. She suggested she has changed her attitude toward children; she'll continue to reevaluate this relationship as well as other relationships as she gets older.

She'll probably mellow. Perhaps as we grow older, we become more aware that giving of ourselves is a big part of being a human being, even if that giving means compromising our own self-centered objectives.

The future will doubtless hold many challenges to marriage. Chain marriage, where a person is married two or three times in a lifetime, is already becoming commonplace. Not only is chain marriage commonplace, but cohabitation, communal living, homosexual marriages, and remaining single are also popular life-styles. The larger cities see many of these patterns first, but then the life-styles spread into smaller communities, challenging the time-honored ideas of what marriage and the family "should" be. Such variations from the standard mold are difficult for many people—and perhaps more difficult for the people involved in them than they, themselves, realize. Many openly aggressive advocates of sexual and life-style freedom have done a total about-face and reverted to more traditional patterns. Many people who have enjoyed one of the newer life-styles have suddenly felt imprisoned by their own choices, wondering where to go next. The resulting confusion is usually frustrating, but then, many marriages are frustrating, too. Traditional marriage, however, has precedent and therefore more stability and familiarity. Even when it's not so good, it's more comfortable than the alternatives.

There is a basic problem with many of the alternatives to the traditional structure of marriage (although these alternatives temporarily serve many individual needs). The problem has to do with the very survival of mankind.

Nurturing children is central to our survival. It's not a matter of choice or what feels good, it's simply a reality. Without children, there is no future; without strong, carefully nurtured children, the future that will result is not worth having. Discussions on what's good for mankind seem rather global when an individual measures a baby against a new car, a trip to Bermuda, or sleeping late on Saturday morning. But the decision to have a child is much different from the determination to buy a dog. The question is far more important than "Am I willing to change its diapers?" or "Can I afford to put him or her through college?" or "Will I like being a parent?" Personal satisfaction is not at all the real issue, although most people who reluctantly have children find more satisfaction than they ever imagined. The issue is the children themselves. The issue is life and the future.

When sexual enjoyment becomes the central focus of interpersonal relationships, it threatens all of us. It is so easy to get caught up in sexual desires, for sex is one of our most basic appetites. The "If it feels good, do it!" attitude has been personally destructive and unfulfilling to many; it has had a disastrous effect on our culture as a whole.

Of course, the interesting alternative life-styles will continue to be the choice of thousands of people. The rational and reasonable choice, however, is one man and one woman in a committed situation. *Committed* is also a crucial word. The one man/one woman arrangement is not any easier than any other arrangement, but it seems to make the most sense, despite the various alternatives we hear of today. The committed man/woman combination provides a stable environment for the growth of a child. It also provides balance and perspective for the child they produce. A child has two chances at getting a very special nurturing love; there is no other love like the love *possible* from a mother or father. Not all children are lucky enough to get this special love; many survive without it. I'm simply talking about the preferable *choice* and the *potential*.

Divorce and chain or sequential marriage deny this optimal environment, although unfortunately, divorce is preferable to many marriages. Homosexual marriages and remaining single also lack the life-nurturing purpose of traditional marriage. The rewards, although different from the rewards of marriage, are no better; they're only different—and usually more difficult in the long run.

I realize my convictions in favor of a one man/one woman marriage are not popular in many circles, and 15 years ago, I would have scoffed at the ideas expressed above, too, dubbing them conservative and therefore pointless. Today, however, I believe the smorgasbord approach to life (look them all over and pick the one you like best) is juvenile and foolhardy. It lacks both perspective and purpose. I'm interested in a better life for both men and women; I'm not interested in women getting as many thrills as they can, forgetting about men and children.

As difficult as it is for women to combine the demands of a home and career, I believe the effort to do anything less is eventually destructive. Only extremists, who have a need for black-and-white answers, are willing to settle for a one-sided choice. The rest of us must deal with the difficulties and rewards on a day-by-day basis, moving steadily toward the balance that will maximize our lives.

As we move toward the maximum balance in marriage, there must be changes. It's neither fair nor possible for a working woman to do as many things for her family as her nonworking grandmother did.

The marriage relationship will be subjected to difficult pressures as we seek the new balance. Men and women must learn to work as a team, when most are uncertain who should be the captain and how the role of captain fluctuates. In a time of rapid change, the fundamentals of life are more important than ever, and the married partners are needed more than ever. There's a wonderful opportunity for individual growth as well as growth in a relationship as we all have more and more to share.

The sharing admittedly becomes more difficult when it involves sharing some of the lesser pleasures in life (like housework), but each succeeding generation will find better answers to the hard battles faced by many. The house of the future will be smaller, simpler, and less demanding. Automation and special services will lighten many of the remaining chores. "The House" will lose much of its sting.

Children will be challenged to take more from two vital parents, being asked to grow more with less. "Less" could, indeed, be more, since many traditional mothers provided a stifling atmosphere for their offspring instead of one that encouraged growth and independence.

Children will be the real winners when they routinely gain a father as well as a mother. As women increasingly find themselves in the workplace, the countermove by men will find them more involved in their powerful role as real fathers. Everyone wins when this happens.

Children also win when they learn to accept more responsibility for taking care of themselves. *Self*-respect is basic, and is gained as humans learn the power of taking care of themselves in all ways.

It's interesting to note that this pertains to mom and dad as well as to children. Women gain more self-respect as they realize they truly *can* support themselves, and men gain more self-respect when they discover the pleasure and dignity of nurturing a child. As Tom Hayden, one of the most outspoken radicals of the 1960s, stated: "Being a father is the most enjoyable and moving experience of my whole life."[*]

The future will be an exciting one. The new adventures may sometimes be difficult, but the results will be invigorating for those men and women willing to face the change directly. The cold statistics reflect the change that is already here, and the forecasters can draw some fairly accurate pictures of the additional changes and reactions that are sure to be a part of our future.

The business world *will* accept women, because they have decided to stay. Women will enter the working world in increasing numbers and will continue to demonstrate that they can be an extremely valuable addition. In many cases, management will realize that women are an invaluable resource, as much a working complement to their male colleagues as the men are a working complement to them. The bottom line will be increased productivity—and *that* is the name of the game!

At home, the relationship between men and women will become routine, but the routine will differ from the traditional model. Role sharing

[*] "Political Bedfellows," *People Weekly*, May 24, 1982, p. 41.

is already more evident in younger couples than it was in their parents' generation, and this sharing will continue until much of the current antagonisms become a thing of the past. Men and women will learn to look forward—but forward in the same direction instead of in opposite directions. It won't be easy, but together they can and will move toward a better, more balanced future for everyone.

11

KEEPING YOUR BALANCE WHILE JUGGLING CHOICES

Living life one day at a time, as we must, makes it very difficult for us to maintain a perspective on ourselves. We easily get out of focus, out of balance with our own view of reality versus reality as it truly is. We are small cogs in such a mass society that, when we blink, we lose our place. The unfortunate result is getting caught up in ourselves; we draw inward, moving daily toward greater and greater confusion about ourselves and our purpose.

There is no doubt that the balance between the individual and the society is one of the greatest questions challenging mankind. Philosophers have contemplated this question since the beginning of time, and we are still left with no clear answer. In America, the traditional focus has been on the individual, resulting in numerous problems for the society as a whole. In the Soviet Union, the traditional focus has been on the society, resulting in numerous problems for its individual members. Both countries are caught in a continual effort to arrive at a better balance, alternating (depending upon who's in power) between a little more or a little less socialism. No country has yet developed the foolproof system, although each new generation believes it has the answers.

As individuals, we do not contemplate complex political/social systems on a daily basis. We have enough trouble getting our own act together. How do we achieve that proper balance in our own lives? How do we measure and live an acceptable balance between our personal needs and the needs of our minisociety, our families, and our communities? There is no absolutely right balance for us that will serve throughout our lives any more than there is an absolutely right balance for all time for society as a whole. We gain some ground, however, simply by realizing that imbalance is what we get most of the time—by smiling and enjoying those bright moments that happen occasionally, those moments when it all seems to hang in there together.

There are some ways, however, to increase the number of days when your life seems in order. It's naive to believe each day can be perfect, but it's optimistic to plan for each day to be more so. I believe you can increase the number of these nearly perfect days by paying close attention to the balance in your life. I have divided these balances into three categories:

Mind/body/spirit
Two sides of the coin
Beginning/middle/end

MIND / BODY / SPIRIT

I have been involved in both women's issues and time management for years. Goal setting is an important part of both topics, and I have always felt women (and men) should set goals for themselves in eight aspects of life. These aspects are:

Career/vocation
Family/friends
Spiritual/religious
Self-development/mental/educational
Health/physical development
Social/civic/community
Leisure/recreational
Wealth/material possessions

I still believe it is important for anyone to give some time to considering his or her personal goals in each of these eight areas. Goal setting is always a useful activity.

But whenever I performed this exercise, I discovered that I *needed* to identify goals in all areas. I felt out of balance if I didn't approach an equal number of goals in each category. I found myself mentally dividing my day into eight sections. Realizing that this wouldn't work, I'd try dividing my week into eight sections. That worked a little better, but there was still far more for me to handle than time comfortably permitted. I felt as though

I were on a treadmill, although I knew the activities that filled my time were, by my own definition, important to me.

One day, while taking a walk (under the "health/physical development" category), I realized I had been trying to juggle too many balls. A simpler, more effective way for me to get more from my life through a balanced approach involves a good balance between attention to my mind, my body, and my spirit. From this foundation, all other categories in my life seemed to fall into place. That walk turned out to be one of the major changing points in my life.

I realized that my personal balance in regard to mind/body/spirit was drastically biased toward activities of the mind. I love to read, think, and talk about intellectual issues. I never believe learning or interacting with people on any level is a waste of time. Heady activities are my ball park and will probably always be my favorite way to spend my time.

The more I thought about this issue, however, the more I realized that intellectual activity is a never ending exercise, going nowhere without a spiritual context to provide structure and direction. Without time for developing your spiritual framework, intellectualizing becomes no more than mental gymnastics.

This realization, of course, had a foundation. My religious beliefs became stronger and clearer to me a few years ago. Before that time, religion was a very minimal part of my existence. Once I accepted the presence of my God in my life, many of the questions I formerly found irreconcilable suddenly had meaning. This meaning provided me with a peace I had never known. I found that the more time I gave to my spiritual growth, the more all other aspects of my life developed richer meaning. It was a secret seldom referred to in most personal-growth literature. Most writers, I assume, are afraid to approach the topic for fear of combining religion and business. I feel it must be considered, and carefully so, if any person hopes to truly grow. It is central to personal development; without it, all other activity and thinking merely skirt the crucial issues.

Physical activity was also an issue I had actively avoided. Oh, now and then I'd have dreams of being a tennis star or running in a marathon (those who did such things always looked so tanned and sexy), but I really didn't want to participate in athletic events of any sort. As my husband often joked, "Her idea of physical exercise is to fill the tub, pull the plug, and fight the current!"

But I found I did better when I did something besides sit and read or talk! I found that doing vigorous sit-ups, riding my bike, or walking rapidly, although not the "sexy" sports, got my blood flowing and kept me more faithful to a healthy diet. I found that when I actually ate the foods

I knew I should eat, and cut out the heavy carbohydrates, white flour, and white sugar I knew were harmful to me, I felt 40 percent more awake. When I kept the mechanics of my body in better working order, everything else seemed to be in a better balance.

The "triangle approach" to balancing my life became an important foundation. I view it simply like this:

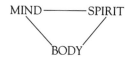

Each point of the triangle supports the other two. Without a strong body, the mind is limited and the spirit less ambitious. Without spiritual development, our thoughts are random pieces of information without context and our physical development an egocentric game. Without a strong mind, our physical activities become more animalistic than human, and our spiritual values border on fanaticism. We need a strong foundation in each of these three areas to give meaning to the other aspects.

Try applying this triangle to your own life. What is your strongest tendency? Do you tend to give more time to mental activities? To physical activities? To spiritual activities? How could you add more balance to your life by giving some thought and time to the other aspects?

I have found it useful to adamantly schedule time for my two weakest areas—spiritual development and physical development. This is not easy to do, for mental activities easily and frequently dominate my day. I have found that getting up a half-hour earlier in the morning gives me time for the sit-ups that get my day off to a good start. Once the blood is flowing, I give 15 to 20 minutes to the matter of my spiritual life. I try to close each day with additional thoughts and reading that improve me spiritually, in addition to consciously remembering the spiritual context of my life during the course of a very busy day. I also sprinkle other physical activities throughout the day. As I said before, one or two walks during the day aid my body as well as my work. They give me the breather I need in addition to the physical movement I require.

Once you have your mind/body/spirit ratio near harmony, you can move to decisions concerning other specifics in your life. Do you want to give the time to friends, civic activities, recreational activities, and so on? Is this the best time in your life to make these additional time commitments, or would another period of your life be better suited? Once you work toward the balance described here, you will be better prepared and more confident about any other decisions you make.

TWO SIDES OF THE COIN

For everything in our lives, there is an opposite that has an equal influence on us. Viewing the black and white of any situation therefore also helps us in our efforts to keep our day-to-day existence in perspective. This thought was expressed beautifully in Ecclesiastes 3:1–8.

A Time for All Things

For everything there is a season, and a time to every purpose under the
    heaven;
A time to be born, and a time to die;
A time to plant, and a time to pluck up that which is planted;
A time to kill, and a time to heal;
A time to break down, and a time to build up;
A time to weep, and a time to laugh;
A time to mourn, and a time to dance;
A time to get, and a time to lose,
A time to keep, and a time to cast away;
A time to rend, and a time to sew;
A time to keep silence, and a time to speak;
A time to love, and a time to hate;
A time of war, and a time of peace.

I try to remember that the low periods of my life are only the other side of the coin. I've had my good times, too. No one gets a 100 percent easy ride, although we sometimes think the other person has a better deal than we do. Then, too, it's only the bad times that give the good times meaning. Up is up only when you compare it to down.

I believe those of us who are working women also have the advantage of balancing a home and a career. (The advantage is the flip side of the problems.) When we have a job, the problems of the home become less intense. When you have a special report to get out, you don't have time to worry about the neighbor's dog that's always chasing your cat. On the other hand, when you have a home and family to occupy you after your workday is finished, you have other things to think about; although that difficult report may still be in the back of your mind, you don't have the time to give it your constant attention. Frequently, the breather away from your urgent situation provides the clue to its resolution. Balance and alternative become useful to you on both fronts.

Finally, it's useful to consider the other, nonfemale view of the world—the male view. Much of what we've talked about in this book has been considered from a woman's perspective. This is necessary because there are many problems and considerations unique to women. However, men *are* one-half of most of our worlds; sometimes their half seems to have more power and influence over us than our own halves. We will gain nothing if we refuse to see important issues from the male viewpoint. Few of us are willing to go as far as to exclude all men from our lives. The few who do aren't going to get very far, because the majority of women *like* having men around. We must therefore work with men to improve our jobs and share the burdens we all feel. Understanding and communications are a big key.

There is another male/female balance that should be acknowledged, although it is usually ignored. All men have some female characteristics, and all women have some male characteristics. Some have more "opposite" characteristics than others. (Tania Harvey was happy to allude to them in her letter in the last chapter.) Many people are uncomfortable with any characteristics that are not traditionally associated with their sex; they are left to fight with the manifestations of opposite-sex characteristics, feeling embarrassed and apologetic.

This issue is particularly tough for women who are moving into a traditionally male world. *Work, business,* and *office* have many leftover male connotations from earlier years, and we must learn to accept the male characteristics that are developed in ourselves as we learn to function in another environment. Fear will do no good. Defensiveness will do no good. Overemphasizing our male characteristics will do no good. The only solution is a healthy acceptance of the other half of ourselves. It is frequently the more unfamiliar half, thus both terrifying and exciting. Again, the balance we achieve is what makes up who we are.

BEGINNING / MIDDLE / END

You will also have a richer life, a more balanced life, if you learn to realize and accept exactly where you are on your life continuum. No one, of course, is guaranteed a full 100 years of life, but that does not keep you from viewing yourself realistically at whatever age you are.

Life has patterns, phases, turning points. Of course, we're all individuals, and no one wants to admit to fitting into a pattern. We thrive on our uniqueness. Most of us hate being put into categories, particularly when we're young. Individuality is the flavor of life, its excitement as well as its challenge.

But most of us would find it beneficial to measure ourselves against those patterns that are most common to the human experience. We are born; we live; we die. The nature of growth calls us to be more developed persons when we are old than when we are young.

Some people, of course, die young. Others fail to mature, getting stuck on "teenager" for 60 years. They never grow beyond self-centeredness, always viewing the world in terms of "What's in it for me?" Even if they reach the age of 80, some people never live a truly full life. They live the same stage over and over again. As soon as a job doesn't go exactly their way they change jobs—or worse yet, give up on their job but continue to collect a pay check. If their spouse no longer pleases their fancy, they get a divorce, find another mate, and try that one for a while. When children force them to trim their personal plans in any way, they decide "Parenthood isn't for me" and leave, emotionally if not physically. They seem afraid to move beyond the beginning stage of life, always starting over in one way or another. They never challenge themselves beyond the superficial.

Perhaps fear plays a large part in this form of getting stuck. If I never really try to develop myself to my potential in all aspects of my skills and relationships, I'll never be disappointed in myself. As long as I find or invent a reason to explain why I accomplished so little, I can always dream I *could* have been or done more, if only. . . . But what if I get to the end and discover I haven't been worth it?

Of course, it's admirable to stay young at heart, no matter how advanced your years. Most of the people I've admired most in my life have been octogenarians who greeted you with a glint in their eye, a perpetual smile on their lips, and a quick kick to their step, even though their walk was a little slow. We should all keep the ability to view life with eagerness and enthusiasm, for life is a continual adventure to enjoy.

And that's why it's disappointing to see so many people "check out before they're done." They fail to experience some of life's greatest blessings as they grow older because they were afraid to let go of the comparatively small pleasures of their youth.

We should also maintain a perspective on our work life as well as on our life in general. Think of your job or career in terms of its past, its present, and its future. Your work, too, is on a continuum. Where is it going? What are your goals? What part has your work life played in your life continuum?

We gain a special balanced perspective on ourselves as we see our life and our actions reflected in those of the people around us. Friends are a beautiful way to view ourselves. As we look back on our lives, we sometimes can remember our friends better (and certainly more objectively) than we remember ourselves. It's important to evaluate the part they played in our lives at that particular time. I very much enjoy three high school friends with whom I have kept in touch throughout the years. We write each other about once a year and see each other once every three to four years. I share, a little, in the variety that is their lives—lives that differ considerably from my own life right now, although twenty years ago we were (at least outwardly) very much alike. I can see the gray hairs and the wrinkles on them a little more readily than I can see them on myself— and it helps me maintain the balance I need to really understand that I'm no longer 16. Our children are now the age we were when we first knew each other; now 16 looks so very young.

Our family members, of all ages, can also help us maintain the balance and perspective we need to see ourselves realistically. Getting to know and respect our grandparents and parents can be a real joy, if only we take the time to do so. Naturally, their opinions differ somewhat from our own; they are products of a different time. But contact with these intimates gives us vital information about where we came from, helping us identify ourselves in a most complicated world.

Our children are our legacy. As Gibran says, "they come through us, but are not of us." They, too, help us see ourselves in the scheme of things. They are frequently the creatures who force us to give up our eternal hopes of youth, for when we care for and support our offspring, nurturing them from infancy to young adulthood, we know our lives have moved down time's continuum. When your child looks you square in the eye and says either "thank you" or "thanks for nothing," you know you're well beyond the beginning stage.

With perspective, we are anchored. This doesn't mean we're immovable; rather, we have a stable foundation and are freed to explore all life has to offer because we know who we are. This perspective also necessitates that we shift our point of view from time to time if we want to cope with it all successfully. What's certain this year becomes a little less certain next year. What was the ideal job when we entered as a trainee becomes swamped with both advantages and disadvantages as the years go by. Our Prince Charming looks a little more froggish on some days than on others. We constantly swing between being more or less contented with our lives and being ready to run away from it all. The truth is, our situation is probably both good for us and bad for us at the same time. The people around us are probably both friends and enemies on the same day.

If we've learned the art of balance and perspective, we'll remember that a rainbow is usually found on those days blessed and cursed with both rain and sunshine. We'll know in our gut that the person who infuriated us on Tuesday may be our biggest asset on Wednesday, and our Prince Charming-turned-toad just may be kissable again on the morrow. With a balanced view, we can know in our hearts that our tears will eventually be relieved with the pleasure of a smile.

12

DISCIPLINE IS THE KEY

DISCIPLINE: A BAD REPUTATION

Bringing our multicolored, complex lives together is not an easy job. Each year we find ourselves with more and more responsibilities, coupled with more and more personal desires. If we are ambitious people, we have many wants, needs, and desires and little time to make them happen. If we are unwilling to give up our personal lives for the sake of our professional lives, we must learn to do what has to be done without hesitation, making each of our actions count.

Decisive action, however, takes personal discipline. That is the special ingredient that makes any system work. Without discipline, our dreams remain just that: dreams, almosts, might-have-beens. We are left with an eternal sense of uneasiness and frustration. We have a continual feeling that someday we'll get it all together, but "someday" never seems to come.

The word *discipline* received a lot of bad press in the 1960s. The mood was one of impulse and spontaneity. We did what felt good. *Discipline* connoted rigidity and form; it seemed opposed to freedom, the freedom we all wanted so desperately.

But we soon found that, with no rules and few guidelines, we went nowhere. Without direction, we ended up running around in circles; we ran in place and found ourselves no nearer our goals one year than we were three years earlier.

DISCIPLINE: THE ANSWER

Discipline *is* the answer. It makes any system work (and, by the way, without it, no system or idea can possibly survive). Discipline means liberation from self-indulgent slavery to self-interest and personal desire. It means the ability to regulate ourselves on the basis of strong principles and beliefs rather than on momentary feelings, impulses, or whims. Discipline does not mean we are no longer warmhearted people. It means, instead, we are free to be truly warmhearted, tempering our tendency to adolescent impulsiveness and sentimentality with wisdom and maturity.

Discipline is forming the right habits that make our lives, day by day, a success instead of a failure. It is that routine which carries us through the hard times that come with greater and greater responsibility. It is, as much as possible, learning to *want* to do what we have to do in order to succeed.

Women today and in the future will need an abundance of discipline if they hope to make a success of their two-pronged lives. There are many exciting challenges, and some will look like battles. Discipline is one of the most powerful allies we have in this personal war.

We must fight the history and alter the tradition that define a simpler role for women. We must be willing to chart a new course, departing from the path followed by our grandmothers. We must work with dedication toward the day when business will fully address the multiple needs of women in the workforce.

Not only will it take discipline to overcome tradition, but it will also take discipline to overcome our own insecurities. A disciplined mind will learn to sort out the difference between what is real and what is perceived in our world. Discipline will conquer the negative attitudes that invade our heads. Discipline will allow us that control over the clock we so desperately need. Courage and discipline to move outward instead of into bed with our insecurities will be the crucial key.

Success on the job front will also call for personal discipline. We won't meet our professional goals with weak-willed hopes and luck. The road to success is full of determination and decisiveness instead of luck. Discipline, strength, chutzpah: These characteristics will determine who ends up on top.

At home, we will need more discipline than ever to maintain happy and healthy families. Our jobs will zap much of our strength and eagerness, and without personal discipline, we will have nothing left for those who actually matter most. We must learn to believe that "The House" is truly a state of mind—and deserves the appropriate amount of attention (that is, not much!). Our relationship with our husbands will also require a particular sort of discipline as this relationship is profoundly affected by the integration of roles we seek. Most of us are secretly aware of our failings in our marital relationship; with discipline, we can begin to do our part in making this primary bond more useful, more supportive to both parties involved.

Discipline serves us and our children at the same time. A disciplined mother and father make for more disciplined children. If children learn discipline at an early age, they will be well prepared for the future. We owe it to our children to insist on the best from them. We owe it to them to show them they don't get anything and everything they want simply because they want it. Through our own discipline, and the discipline we impose upon them, we show them how to accept the waiting for worthwhile results. Discipline is one of the most important legacies we can give to them, and it comes through developing it in ourselves.

DEVELOPING DISCIPLINE

The future belongs to the disciplined. Everyone else will be an also-ran. How do you develop discipline? How do you begin to control yourself when you're so accustomed to living an undisciplined life?

First of all, review your true goals. What do you *really* want? What are you willing to do to get it? Are you willing to make the difficult choices to achieve your goal? Are you really willing to make the sacrifice? Discipline will require that you develop new habits, and the older you are, the more difficult it is to change. If you feel you are sincere in your determination to be more disciplined, define yourself as "married" to your commitment. Be unswerving, at least until your new habits are established.

Second, learn to be careful about personal habits. Leave a room or a situation in better condition than when you found it. Develop a sense of orderliness about your environment. This environment will lay the groundwork for mental orderliness.

Third, schedule some time to train yourself in the art of logical thinking. Read a simplified, but useful book on logic and begin identifying your world in terms of these insights. You will find a sense of order you have never before seen.

Fourth, work on controlling your body when it is out of line. Many of us have "nervous conditions" that continually signal our internal confusion. Stop talking incessantly. Stop biting your fingernails, overeating, chewing gum, drinking coffee, tapping your foot. Practice "calm," both mental and physical.

Fifth, work on being on time. You don't need to be enslaved by the clock to develop the habit of being punctual. When you are consistently on time, you teach those around you that you are a respecter of time and that you would appreciate it if they respected your time as well. Again, you will continue to gain a sense of self-confidence as you find yourself on time instead of continually late.

Sixth, be ready for the unexpected. Expect it every day. Expect difficulties: handle them calmly, with style. Once, over a cup of coffee with a girl friend, we summarized our conversation (which had been filled with soap-opera-type reports of the lives of friends and family) thus: "Icky is a way of life." This sentiment may never end up on a sampler, but it is frequently very true. Life is full of undesirable events. The disciplined person handles them by planning for them as much as possible—and by accepting those unplanned events with peace. The alternative to reacting calmly is finding ourselves in a constant state of turmoil.

Seventh, learn to take criticism objectively. There's probably a message in the criticism, if you could only hear it through your defensiveness. Grow through criticism; learn, too, to consider the source when you are being criticized.

Eighth, learn to take that "pause that refreshes." When you start to make a decision or embark upon an action chosen through emotion or impulse instead of through discipline, stop a moment before you act. *Think* about what you're doing. The difference between eventual success and continual failure is frequently just that pause.

Ninth, act on what you know you should do. Don't sit around considering all the possible ramifications forever. Get the facts, carefully analyze them, and *act* before you analyze things to death.

And finally, realize that life becomes more enjoyable through discipline. As a disciplined person, you are doing the very best you can humanly do. There is no reason to be frustrated and upset with yourself today or any day. You can therefore enjoy each day as it comes, savoring the moment and knowing that it leads to the best possible future for you and your family. The joy in life is the trip, anyway, not the destination.

Courage and discipline are the only alternative to fearful living. We fear many things, from success to tomorrow. When we think about it carefully, we realize the only course we can take is to *crave* the challenge we face. If we do not learn to look eagerly toward the future, we are left wallowing in the way we *think* things used to be. Looking backward (except occasionally on a rainy Sunday afternoon) is a self-destructive activity.

Don't look backward. Instead, paint, embroider, chisel, or burn these words on a sign and hang it where you can see it daily:

LIFE HAS ONE DIRECTION: AHEAD!

Selected Readings

Bolles, Richard Nelson, *What Color Is Your Parachute?* Berkeley, Calif.: Ten Speed Press, 1972.

Douglass, Donna N., "Quick Tips for a Busy Day." Available free by sending a stamped, self-addressed envelope to Quick Tips for a Busy Day, Time Management Center, 7612 Florissant Road, St. Louis, MO 63121.

Douglass, Merrill E., and Donna N. Douglass, *Manage Your Time, Manage Your Work, Manage Yourself.* New York: AMACOM, 1980.

Drucker, Peter F., *The Effective Executive.* New York: Harper & Row, 1967.

Hennig, Margaret, and Anne Jardin, *The Managerial Woman.* Garden City, N.Y.: Doubleday, 1977.

Jones, William M., and Ruth A. Jones, *Two Careers—One Marriage.* New York: AMACOM, 1980.

Killian, Ray A., *The Working Woman: A Male Manager's View.* New York: AMACOM, 1971.

McConkey, Dale, *No-Nonsense Delegation.* New York: AMACOM, 1974.

Pinkstaff, Marlene Arthur, and Anna Bell Wilkinson, *Women at Work: Overcoming the Obstacles.* Reading, Mass.: Addison-Wesley, 1979.

Scarf, Maggie, *Unfinished Business: Pressure Points in the Lives of Women.* Garden City, N.Y.: Doubleday, 1980.

Scott, Dru, *How to Put More Time in Your Life.* New York: Rawson, Wade, 1980.

Sheehy, Gail, *Pathfinders.* New York: William Morrow, 1981.

Stewart, Nathaniel, *The Effective Woman Manager.* New York: Wiley, 1978.

Swart, J. Carroll, *A Flexible Approach to Working Hours.* New York: AMACOM, 1978.

Winston, Stephanie, *Getting Organized.* New York: Norton, 1978.

Index